A BREEZE
FROM
THE GULF

Plays by Mart Crowley

The Boys in the Band (1968)
Remote Asylum (1970)
A Breeze from the Gulf (1973)

Mart Crowley

A BREEZE
FROM
THE GULF

Farrar, Straus and Giroux / New York

Copyright © 1974 by Mart Crowley
All rights reserved
First printing, 1974
Printed in the United States of America
Published simultaneously in Canada
by Doubleday Canada Ltd., Toronto
Designed by Marion Hess

Library of Congress Cataloging in Publication Data

Crowley, Mart.
  A breeze from the gulf.
  A play.
  I. Title.
PS3553.R6B7   1974   812'.5'4   73–21901

To my mother and my father

A Breeze from the Gulf was first produced on the New York stage by Charles Hollerith Jr., and Barnard S. Straus at the Eastside Playhouse on October 15, 1973. The scenery was designed by Douglas W. Schmidt, the lighting by Ken Billington, and the costumes by Stanley Simmons. The play was directed by John Going.

The original cast was:

LORAINE	*Ruth Ford*
TEDDY	*Scott McKay*
MICHAEL	*Robert Drivas*

A BREEZE
FROM
THE GULF

Characters

LORAINE   the mother

TEDDY   the father

MICHAEL   the son

*The play is in two acts representing the passage of ten years—
1950 to 1960.*

*The scenery should consist simply of levels and stairs of varied
and interesting heights, with only the most basic and essential
set and hand props employed to identify a playing area as a
particular room or place, or as an exterior locale.*

*Much of the action takes place in the Connelly home, the basic
level representing the living room, another the kitchen, three
others three bedrooms in which there are only three simple
beds. Whenever the action occurs away from the Connelly
home—on the beach, in an institution, in a hospital, in a coastline bar, a "screen drop" consisting of three separate panels
flies in to mask the three permanent beds.*

MICHAEL *is to be portrayed by an actor of mature compre-
hension, yet one who physically belongs to that vague period
between puberty and manhood. Within the convention of the
play he must communicate an age range from fifteen to twenty-
five years old. Because of the convention of the play, because
he "remembers" the other two characters, he is outside of time,
even though he appears in the scenes. Therefore, with the ex-
ception of an ordinary bathrobe, I would like him costumed in
a dark-blue suit, a dark-blue necktie, and a beige raincoat
throughout. Of course, he doesn't wear all the garments at the
same time all of the time. Sometimes he wears only his under-
shorts, and other times he may wear the suit trousers and his
shirt with the sleeves rolled up and the collar open. It depends
on the age he is playing and the context of the scene.*

LORAINE *and* TEDDY, *the other two characters, change both
costumes and makeup in accordance with the requirements and
chronology of the material.*

Although this play takes place in the state of Mississippi, I do not want it to drip with magnolias. Hence, only LORAINE *speaks with a Southern accent.* MICHAEL *is basically a stranger in a foreign country from the very beginning, and* TEDDY's *speeches and the jargon employed will, hopefully, take care of his origins and current environment.*

ACT 1

Scene 1

As the houselights dim, MICHAEL's *silhouette appears, slowly tracing a path from bed to bed, from level to level, finally emerging through the panels of the screen drop, to be picked up by a spotlight as he comes down to the stage apron.*

LORAINE

    [Offstage]

MIIICHAEL! OHHHH, MIIIIIICHAELLLLLLL!

    [A light comes up on LORAINE, *standing on the opposite side of the stage, calling . . . out front]*

MIIIICHAEL! Come on inside, honey, and look at the house.
—Oh, Michael!

MICHAEL

    [After a pause, out front]

Yeeeeessuuuuummmmmmm.

    *[*MICHAEL *removes his suit jacket and his necktie, unbuttons his shirt collar, pulls the shirttail out, starts to roll up his sleeves and kick off his loafers]*

LORAINE

    [Turns to face him]

Come on inside and see the front room.

    *[*MICHAEL *turns slowly to face her but doesn't leave his position]*

Stop that runnin'! Just slow up!

MICHAEL

    [Still standing in place]

Yessum.

LORAINE
[*Exasperated*]

Ohh, Michael, how many times do I have to tell you, *don't run!*
[MICHAEL *now begins to move, walking slowly toward* LORAINE *as she speaks*]

I sound like a broken record. Don't run, don't run, don't run, don't run . . .

MICHAEL
I know better than to run.

LORAINE
You're just wringin' wet with perspiration! You're gonna have the croup tonight just as sure as shootin'!

MICHAEL
P-U! It stinks in here.

LORAINE
No wonder—there hasn't been a breath of fresh air in here in twenty years. Did you notice the roof? Don't you just love it—terra-cotta tile.

MICHAEL
And there's a triple-car garage!

LORAINE
They must have had automobiles to let! Oh boy, oh boy, I sure hope your daddy's gettin' warm after all the buildin' up I've been doin'. After all the times I've been drivin' by this place watchin' and watchin' that old "for sale" sign. I've just gotta think of a way to convince him.

MICHAEL
Maybe if we say an "Our Father" real hard, it'll help.

LORAINE
Well, you pray and I'll think.

MICHAEL
No. You have to pray too or else it won't work.

LORAINE
[*Sighs*]
Well, anything's worth a try.
[*Looks heavenward*]
Please, dear God. For God's sake, don't trouble the water when I'm just gettin' a bite.
[TEDDY *raps "shave-and-a-haircut-two-bits" and enters, dressed in a suit and tie and wearing a hat*]

MICHAEL
Daddy!

TEDDY
[*To* MICHAEL]
Hello, Joe, whadda-ya know!

MICHAEL
Just got back from the picture show!

LORAINE
[*Ignoring* TEDDY]
Where's the real-estate man?

TEDDY
[*Removing his hat*]
Good afternoon. How are you today, you yummy tootsie-wootsie.

LORAINE
[*To* MICHAEL]
I'm married to a clown.
[*To* TEDDY]
Teddy, be serious. Where's the real-estate man?

TEDDY
He's not coming.

LORAINE
Not comin'! I don't believe it!

TEDDY
Would I shit a blind girl?

LORAINE
Honey, don't talk that way in front of your son. Lord only knows what language he'll grow up to use.

TEDDY
[*To* MICHAEL]
Oh, I beg your pardon.

LORAINE
What went wrong?

TEDDY
It's already been sold.
[*Silence. A pause. Then he pulls a set of keys from his pocket and jingles them*]
Santy Claus!

LORAINE
—Oh, honey! I don't believe it! Oh my stars!
[*And she rushes to him and throws her arms around his neck*]

MICHAEL
Oh-boy-oh-boy-oh-boy!

LORAINE
[*Hugging* TEDDY *ecstatically*]
You devil you!

TEDDY
I just hope it makes you happy.

LORAINE
Happy! I've never been so happy in all my life!

MICHAEL
Me too! Me too! Me too! Me too!
[*He rushes to embrace the two of them as they embrace each other*]

LORAINE
[*To* TEDDY]
You're happy too, aren't you?

TEDDY
[*Breaks away gently*]
You know me, Mama. I don't really care. To me, it's an awful lot of show. But if it's what you and Michael want, that's all that matters.

LORAINE
[*Sincerely*]
Oh, honey, thank you.
[*She kisses him, turns to* MICHAEL]
You know, I just knew we were goin' to get this place. I knew it from the moment I asked the man why the livin'-room floor sagged in the middle and he said it was from so much dancin'

at so many parties! He said one night at a party everybody was high as Georgia pines doin' the Charleston when suddenly the whole thing dropped four inches and they had to go into the basement and prop it up. But once they did, everybody picked up where they left off and never skipped a beat! Well. I knew I liked this house and this house liked me.

TEDDY
Are you planning on doing some entertaining?

LORAINE
Of course I'm not. You know I've never been one for socializin'. Thank God, we don't have any friends so we won't *have* to entertain. But that's what this house was built for. This livin' room is more like a ballroom. Imagine! Eleven doors in four walls!

MICHAEL
And some of them seem to go nowhere.

LORAINE
But you'll notice most of them go to the porches all around. People must have just danced out through one and had a cigarette and danced right back in through another! I suppose we can seal up some of the dead ends—like that botched-up affair that covers the old built-in bar.

MICHAEL
[*Disappointed*]
Awww, the bar is my favorite!

LORAINE
I wonder who you get that from.

TEDDY
Tear it out! I don't care. I'll have my toddies in the kitchen anyway.

MICHAEL
[*At the bar*]
It's even got a built-in radio!

LORAINE
I'm just gonna stucco over that whole space.

MICHAEL
And it still works! Listen!
[*"The Very Thought of You" starts to play.* TEDDY *starts to sing along* . . . TEDDY *grabs* LORAINE *and starts to dance*]

TEDDY
". . . the little ordinary things that everyone ought to do. I see your face in every flower, your eyes in skies . . ."

MICHAEL
[*Interrupts their dance*]
What do you suppose this is?
[TEDDY *gives up—walks away*]

LORAINE
Oh! It's an ice shaver!

TEDDY
In case your ice has got five o'clock shadow at 3 A.M.

MICHAEL
[*Singing*]
Shave-and-a-haircut-two-bits!

LORAINE
[*To* MICHAEL]
It's to shave ice for frozen daiquiris and silver fizzes.

MICHAEL
First time I've ever seen one.

LORAINE
The first time I ever saw one was in the bar of the Edgewater Gulf Hotel in Biloxi. Remember, Daddy? Or was it the bar in the Palmettos? Well, it was on the coast somewhere. Sure never saw one till I saw you.

MICHAEL
Ouuuu! There's a dead mouse in the sink.

TEDDY
He's probably just passed out. Run a little water on him—maybe he'll come to.

LORAINE
Don't touch him! He's probably riddled with disease. That's where that ghastly odor is comin' from.

MICHAEL
[*To* TEDDY]
I'm afraid he's a goner.

TEDDY
Cirrhosis strikes again!

LORAINE
Open a door! Let's open all the doors! Let's let the sunset in!
[*She and* MICHAEL *open what would be all the doors to the porches and the light changes*]

MICHAEL

Open sesame.

TEDDY

Now we got two nigger maids: Willy Mae and sesame.

LORAINE

Isn't it glorious! I know just how I'm gonna fix it up. I'm gonna paint everything green.

TEDDY

Well, I love green.

LORAINE

I don't mean Kelly green—a rich green, a luscious forest green with brilliant white enamel woodwork.
  [*To* MICHAEL]
And I'm gonna do our bedroom in wallpaper of giant cabbage roses. I can see it now.

TEDDY

I can see you're gonna put me back in the poorhouse.

MICHAEL

Don't I get to have a bedroom of my own now?

LORAINE

Whatever for?

MICHAEL

Mama, I'm fifteen years old—it's beginning to make me nervous.

LORAINE

  [*Reflectively*]
You know, although I'm a Southerner, I'm glad we didn't try

and buy any of those antebellum or mainline magnolia homes. I think you really have to be aristocracy to live in them. Of course, I can put up a good front right along with the best of 'em if I have to—but I don't think I have to here. I feel like this house has just been sittin' here waitin' here for me.

MICHAEL

Daddy, are you considered a rebel, being born in St. Louis?

LORAINE

No, honey. Missouri's not in the South! Missouri's not even in the North. Missouri's nowhere.

TEDDY
  [*To* MICHAEL]
In answer to your question, I am from what is known by most intelligent people as the Midwest. Your mother never heard of it.

LORAINE

You know, your daddy and I were always livin' in the spirit of this place even if we *were broke* and livin' out of suitcases and taxicabs.

TEDDY
  [*To* MICHAEL]
You were too little to remember it, but once we drove past the hotel where you were born and I said, "Look, baby, that's where Jesus brought you." And you looked up at me and said, "Did he bring me in a taxi?"

LORAINE
  [*In her own world*]
I'm so beside myself with joy, I feel like doin' a dance!
  [LORAINE *takes* MICHAEL *and starts to dance*]

TEDDY
Well, let's do one.

[*Pushes* MICHAEL *away*]

Turn up the music, son.

[MICHAEL *turns up the volume on the radio. "Deep Purple" is playing.* TEDDY *joins* LORAINE *in the middle of the floor, puts his left hand up to her right one, and wraps his right arm around her spine to rest his palm on her behind. She reaches back, slaps his hand, pushes it up to the small of her back*]

LORAINE
Come on, Daddy. Don't act dirty.

TEDDY
Oh, excuse me. I thought I was dancing with the aristocracy.

LORAINE
You've had a drink, haven't you?

TEDDY
Just a little toddy to be somebody.

LORAINE
I know it's the truth. You can't fool me.

TEDDY
I'm not trying to.

LORAINE
Well, let's not argue about it now. I'm too happy. I don't know why, but I feel like, at long last, we've come home!

TEDDY
Heaven is *my* home.

LORAINE

Well, I don't know about you, but *I* am *in* heaven!
[*She exits*]

TEDDY
[*Surveys the house, slaps and rubs his hands together in a gesture of luck as if he has a pair of dice; rolls them as he speaks out front*]
Oh Lawdy, Lawdy! I wonder what the po' folks are doin' tonight!
[MICHAEL *continues to dance as the light fades, but a spot stays on him. Music fades; he stops, a pause, puts hands in his pockets, reflects for a moment . . .*]

Scene 2

An automobile horn toots "shave-and-a-haircut-two-bits."

MICHAEL
   [*Out front singsongs*]
Daddy's home!

   [*A light comes up on* TEDDY *in the kitchen area holding a
   brown paper bag behind his back*]

TEDDY
   [*To* MICHAEL]
Santy Claus!

MICHAEL
I've been waiting up for you— Did you bring a sack?

TEDDY
   [*Flatly*]
Aren't you even gonna say hello?

MICHAEL
Hello-did-you-bring-a-sack?

TEDDY
Where's that blond woman I live with?

MICHAEL
Upstairs lying down. What'd you bring?

LORAINE
[*Offstage*]
Yoo-hoo!

TEDDY
Who you yoo-hooin'?

LORAINE
[*Entering*]
I'm yoo-hooing you! Aren't you gonna say hello to *me*?

TEDDY
Hello, you.
[*He attempts to kiss her, she turns away.* MICHAEL *sees the paper bag*]

MICHAEL
[*Elated*]
You brought one!

TEDDY
[*To* LORAINE]
What's the matter—my breath bad?

LORAINE
No, indeed. You smell sweet—like always. You always smell just like orange juice.

TEDDY
That's just my natural fragrance. You sure look pretty tonight.

LORAINE
Why, thank you.

MICHAEL
What'd you bring?

LORAINE
[*To* MICHAEL]
Oh, honey, let the man get in the door!

MICHAEL
I want to know what's in the sack tonight!

TEDDY
Some real good ham—sliced thin as a whistle. Some Wisconsin
cheese and some Swiss. You want some?

MICHAEL
Uh-uh.

TEDDY
Say, no sir, don't gimme any of that uh-uh business.

MICHAEL
No sir.

LORAINE
He couldn't eat another thing—we just got in awhile ago. We
went to Ambrosiani's and he had spaghetti.

MICHAEL
Smell *my* breath.

LORAINE
I had saltimbocca alla Romana.

TEDDY
Oh.

LORAINE
I told you I was gonna take him there this Saturday.

TEDDY

I forgot.

[*To* MICHAEL]

—And I brought you some new movie magazines.

MICHAEL

Oh boy!

[TEDDY *takes the magazines out of the bag, hands them to* MICHAEL, *puts the bag on the kitchen table*]

LORAINE

[*To* MICHAEL]

Let me see! Let me see who's on the covers!—Oh, I can't stand *her*.

[*Flips to another magazine*]

Oh, I love *him*.

[*Flips to another*]

Oh, I can't stand *her*.

TEDDY

The score is two to one. The girls lose.

[*Meanwhile,* TEDDY *has proceeded to empty his pockets of their contents—money, glasses, pill bottles, leaflets, keys, and lastly, his rosary with which he reverently makes the sign of the cross and then places it with the other things on the table*]

LORAINE

[*Picking up a leaflet*]

What's this?

TEDDY

A pamphlet on the Immaculate Conception.

LORAINE

Oh.

TEDDY

I know—you can't stand *her.*

LORAINE

Honey!

TEDDY

   [*Goes to* LORAINE]
How do you feel?

LORAINE

   [*Pulling away*]
Pretty good. I've had a little old naggin' headache all day—but other than that I'm O.K.
   [*Moving toward the kitchen counter*]
Think I'll just take another one of my pills.
   [*She gets a glass of water and a bottle of pills and takes one*]
You look tired.

TEDDY

It's not that I'm so tired, it's just that my damn ankles have begun to swell up so much.
   [*He loosens his tie; places his jacket on the back of a chair*]

LORAINE

It's from standin' on your feet long hours. How are things at the place?

TEDDY

Hand over fist. I only hope the good Lord will let it hold out till I can get the building paid for and the last note on this house. Then we'll really be in clover.
   [*He has taken a bottle of gin out of the paper bag.* LORAINE *reacts unfavorably as he picks up a glass and pours himself a drink*]

LORAINE
[*Picking up the empty sack with disdain, throwing it away.
Moving off*]
They say it may snow.

MICHAEL
Just think! Wouldn't it be wonderful if we had snow for
Christmas this year!

TEDDY
Well, if my in-laws show up, I can guarantee a little frost.

LORAINE
[*Bristling*]
Well, they'll be here!

TEDDY
In-laws and outlaws!

LORAINE
If you had any family left, I'm sure they'd be right here on
top of us too!

MICHAEL
Daddy, does it snow a lot in St. Louis?

TEDDY
All the time. Why, I can remember when I was your age, my
Aunt Maureen having to break the ice in the water pitcher
before she could wash her face. She always made me stay in
the bed till she got up and lit the stove and *heated* the water
for me.

MICHAEL
[*Lamely*]
Where was your . . . Uncle Brian?

LORAINE

Out drunk somewhere, no doubt.

TEDDY

Probably.

MICHAEL
    [*Rather distantly*]
I remember it was cold the night you threw Uncle Brian out
of our old house.

LORAINE

That was too good for him—that dirty old s.o.b.—I went by
the funeral parlor today to see Dr. Valkenberg and his Mexican
matador. What a scandal *that's* been. It has just rocked this
town. They found strychnine in the bottle of wine they were
drinkin'—so it was murder as well as suicide.

TEDDY

That's too fancy for me.

LORAINE

You should have seen them. They looked just like wax. I declare, they were the most gorgeous corpses I've ever seen!

TEDDY

Sounds creepy to me.

LORAINE

I always liked Dr. Valkenberg. I was always sorry he wasn't
a gynecologist so I could have tried him out. He was so nice to
me when I was out to the hospital to have my partial hysterec-
tomy. But you know and I know I could never leave Dr.
LaSalle. He's just like a father to me.

TEDDY

I was thinking this year we might go to the Sugar Bowl game for Christmas.

MICHAEL

You mean go to New Orleans?

TEDDY

How would you like that, Mama?

LORAINE

You know me! I just love to travel! Boy, howdy! If I had my way, I'd keep one foot in the middle of the big road.

TEDDY

Well, I think we ought to try and plan on it. We could go to the track, have some good food, maybe take in a stage show, and see the game on New Year's Day.

LORAINE

[*To* MICHAEL]
I know you'll adore the clubhouse at the race track. It's not just like bein' *at* a movie, it's like bein' *in* a movie!

TEDDY

[*To* MICHAEL]
I can't see it myself. Stuck off to one side with those stuckups, when you can have box seats right down on the finish line!

LORAINE

[*Remembering. Deflated*]
Oh.—What'll I do about Hattiebeth?

TEDDY

All you have to do is write to her and politely inform her and her husband that we have other plans this Christmas.

LORAINE
I hope she won't get her nose out of joint.

TEDDY
Why are you bothered about what those heathens think!

LORAINE
[*Bluntly*]
Listen, Teddy, regardless of what you think of my sister and her husband, they have been damned nice to us.

TEDDY
I never did like that goddamn baby carriage!

MICHAEL
What baby carriage?

LORAINE
Your baby carriage! If it hadn't been for Aunt Hattiebeth and the Captain, we'd have been pushin' you in a wheelbarrow!

TEDDY
[*Unlacing his shoes*]
And, Jesus, I'll never hear the end of it.

MICHAEL
Don't fight. Please.

TEDDY
We're not fighting.

LORAINE
Do you have to undress in the kitchen and empty your pockets out all over creation!
[*Gathering up the articles on the table*]
Michael, take your daddy's things up to his room.

TEDDY
Can't I even relax in my own kitchen?

LORAINE
No.

TEDDY
Why not?

LORAINE
Because if your ankles are swollen, what you need is to elevate them. What you need is to lie down. So, come on, I'll turn down your bed.
[*She takes his coat and his hat and exits*]

TEDDY
What I need is my head examined for putting up with this. I wonder what a psychiatrist would say.

LORAINE
[*Going up the stairs*]
That you're crazy in the head.
[MICHAEL *has put* TEDDY's *things in* TEDDY's *bedroom.* LORAINE *enters, puts his coat and hat down, and starts to turn down the bed with* MICHAEL's *help*]

TEDDY
[*Picking up his shoes and his drink and heading for the stairs*]
Did I tell you the joke about the cripple who went to the psychiatrist?—Well, this one cripple was telling this other one that he'd been to a psychiatrist to see if the reason he couldn't walk was because it was all in his head.
[*He stops on a step; has a sip of his drink*]
So the other one said, "So, what happened?" And the first

cripple said, "Well, the psychiatrist said there's only one way to find out—throw away your crutches and take a step!"

[*He resumes ascending the stairs*]

So the other one said, "So then what happened?" And the first cripple said, "Well, then I threw away my right crutch." And the other one said, "So then what happened?" And the cripple said, "And then I threw away my left crutch." And the other one said, "And then what happened?"

[*He appears in the bedroom*]

And the first cripple said, "And then I fell on my fucking face!"

[MICHAEL *starts to giggle.* LORAINE *starts to snicker, then laughs out loud as* TEDDY *starts to laugh, sets his glass down, and pushes* LORAINE *over onto the bed with him.* MICHAEL *collapses from the other side and the three of them lie in a heap, roaring with laughter. Finally,* LORAINE *sits up, wiping tears from her face*]

LORAINE

[*Still through a few guffaws*]

. . . Oh! . . . that is the funniest thing I ever heard—my headache is just killin' me!

[*Her laughter dies away; she kisses* TEDDY]

Good night, honey.

[*She gets up and goes to her room and lies in a seductive pose on her bed, allowing the slit of her negligee to part and reveal her legs*]

MICHAEL

[*Crawls up and kisses* TEDDY]

Good night, Daddy.

[MICHAEL *goes to his bedroom, removes his shirt and pants, and gets into bed as* TEDDY *calls to him*]

TEDDY

Good night, son. Are you going to Holy Communion in the morning?

MICHAEL
Yes sir.

TEDDY
Well remember, don't have anything to eat or drink afterward until you swallow a few sips of water—in case any of the sacred host remains in your mouth. You hear?

MICHAEL
Yes sir.

LORAINE
[*From her bed*]
Good night, darlin'.

MICHAEL
[*From his bed*]
Good night, Mama.

LORAINE
I love you.

MICHAEL
I love you too.

TEDDY
[*From his bed*]
I love you three.
> [*And he takes the pamphlet and glasses out of his coat pocket, puts the glasses on, starts to read and sip his drink as the lights dim out on him and* LORAINE *while a spot holds on* MICHAEL. *Pause. The sound of the Gulf surf comes up.* MICHAEL *gets out of bed, picks up a beach towel, and comes center as the screen drop flies in . . .*]

Scene 3

A light picks up TEDDY *in beach clothes and dark glasses. He has a pair of binoculars on a strap around his neck.*

TEDDY

[*Looking off through the binoculars*]
Get set. Here she comes.

MICHAEL
I'm ready. Are you ready?

TEDDY
Yeah, yeah, now remember, don't say a word and for Jesus' sake, don't laugh.

MICHAEL
I won't laugh. Don't *you* laugh.

TEDDY
Don't worry about me.

LORAINE
Teddy?

TEDDY
Now, hurry up! Here she comes.
[MICHAEL *puts an arm around* TEDDY's *neck and hops into his arms. Once* TEDDY *is holding him,* MICHAEL *releases his grip and bends backward, letting his head and arms dangle as his feet do*]

LORAINE
[*Offstage*]
What's goin' on? What're y'all doin'? Teddy?
[TEDDY *has a glazed expression and moves forward a step at a time.* MICHAEL *allows his head to wobble as* LORAINE *darts on stage wearing beach clothes and carrying a Kodak*]
Teddy, what happened? What's wrong? ANSWER ME!
[*Simultaneously on cue,* MICHAEL *flips up and . . .*]

TEDDY and MICHAEL
BOO!!!

LORAINE
[*Recoils with fright, then recovers*]
. . . You bastards!
[TEDDY *and* MICHAEL *fall to the ground, laughing*]
. . . I've told you not to do that to me!

MICHAEL
Oh, Mama, not again!

TEDDY
[*To* MICHAEL, *with his arm around him*]
You see! What'd I tell you—she fell for it again! What a sucker you are, Loraine!

LORAINE
[*Furious*]
Because I'm always terrified somethin' has really happened to my child!

MICHAEL
I'm not a child any more.

LORAINE
I don't care if you're seventy! You'll always be my baby!

TEDDY
[*Shaking his head, patting* MICHAEL]
She fell for it again! I don't believe it!
[LORAINE *picks up the towel, which has fallen on the ground, and goes to put it around* MICHAEL's *shoulders. He does not see her at first, is startled by her proximity, and flinches*]

LORAINE
Watcha flinchin' for? You thought I was gonna pop you one, didn't you? 'Cause you know you need it. Here.
[*Pulling* MICHAEL *away from* TEDDY]
Put this towel around your shoulders. You're gonna get blistered and make yourself sick.

MICHAEL
[*Dully*]
Let's go for a walk.

TEDDY
Good deal. Let's walk a ways so Mama can cool off. She's mighty hot under the collar.

LORAINE
I rue the day you ever floated down the Mississippi! I should have taken one look at you and run for dear life in the other direction!

[*Pause. They stroll*]

TEDDY
Look, Loraine!

LORAINE
What?

TEDDY

That big open space over yonder.

LORAINE

That empty lot across the highway?

TEDDY

Yeah.

LORAINE

Well, I see it. What about it?
    [Gasps]
Oh my goodness! Oh my goodness gracious!

TEDDY

Ain't that somethin'!

MICHAEL

What?

LORAINE

That's where the Palmettos was! Have you ever! What happened, Teddy? Did a hurricane get it?

TEDDY

I don't know. Maybe they tore it down.

LORAINE

Gone! Oh, that just gets away with me so!

TEDDY

I'm just as glad it's gone.

LORAINE

Oh, Daddy, how can you say that?

TEDDY

I'm glad those days are over and done with.

MICHAEL

What was it like?

LORAINE

Well, from the outside it appeared to be one of the most swell-elegant private residences along this entire coastline. But inside it was the swankiest casino on the Gulf of Mexico. Your daddy and I worked there years ago. My God, Teddy, what do you suppose ever became of Clayton?

TEDDY

Who knows?

MICHAEL

Who?

LORAINE

Clayton Reed. The Reed brothers. There were three of them— Clayton and Ramsey and Bubber Reed. And they were all the best-lookin' things you ever laid eyes on. And rich as Croesus!

TEDDY

I always thought maybe you took a shine to Clayton.

LORAINE

I did no such a thing! Clayton was my favorite and that's all there was to it!

[*To* MICHAEL]

They were born gamblers—had it in their blood just like your daddy. That's why they got along so well.

TEDDY

We got along because they trusted me. Clayton knew if they were gonna be successful crooks, they needed an honest crook to help 'em.

LORAINE

The story was that they had won the Palmettos in a poker game, but no one knew for sure. Daddy and I had just been married and I wasn't dry behind the ears. I used to hang around the bar late at night, playin' the slot machines, waitin' for Daddy to get off—when one night Clayton came up to me and said, "Lollie, you sure are a pretty thing. How'd you like to make a little somethin' on the side?" And I said, "Doin' what, I'd like to know." And he told me. And the next day he took me in this limousine to the best shop in Biloxi and bought me a lime-green evenin' dress. I'll never forget it as long as I live. He did all the talkin'—said, "We'd like to be shown the finest dinner dresses you have." And with that they brought out the most gorgeous clothes I've ever seen in my life. One after another—satin and beaded and spangles, and I was just ga-ga! But Clayton didn't react to a single thing until they showed us this one made of lime-green crepe de chine with no trim on it at all. And then he said, "Lollie, why don't you try on that one." And I did. It had kind of a flared skirt and long, full, full puff sleeves that hung down and were gathered up by a band at the wrists. And it was high in the front and had no back at all. And I floated out of the dressin' room like green smoke. And Clayton said, "We'll take it!" I asked him why he had chosen that particular one. He said, "Because it was the simplest and the most dignified—and because of those big, beautiful sleeves. I hope you like it." And I said, "I think it was my favorite all along and I just never knew it till you told me."

MICHAEL
Was that your job?

LORAINE
I was the shill. Clayton said people would watch my good looks rather than the dice and so they gave me money to play with and I stood on the left side of Daddy, who was ridin' the stick. On a big bet I would place a chip on the field, and my big, beautiful sleeve would spread on the board and cover Daddy's hand as he switched dice. God! We had nerve in those days! I did that time and time again and never batted a beaded eyelash, and now it scares me just to think of it.

TEDDY
Oh yeah, I think you were stuck on Clayton all right.

LORAINE
Oh, honey, he didn't mean a thing to me. I liked him like a father. He was so reserved and genteel.

MICHAEL
What ever became of him?

LORAINE
Well, Clayton just played out and picked up and moved on. No one has seen nor heard of him since. That's one thing in this life—we never know what will happen to us.

TEDDY

[*Looking through the binoculars*]
Look at what's become of that big old place over there.

LORAINE

I can see a cross above the porch, but what does the sign say?

TEDDY

Retreat House.

LORAINE

Is that like a monastery?

TEDDY

Yeah. But more. Michael, tell your mama what a retreat house is.

MICHAEL

It's a place where you can sort of be a monk for a day. Or two days or a week, depending on how long the retreat lasts. For ladies I guess it's like temporarily taking the veil. You read and meditate and listen to talks and keep a vow of silence. I don't think you'd like it.

LORAINE

Do you have to abstain from alcohol?

TEDDY

I would never drink while making a retreat.

LORAINE

Then I'm all for your makin' one.

TEDDY
It would defeat the point. I'd take a pledge—I'd promise God that I wouldn't drink.

MICHAEL
For how long?

TEDDY
Well, certainly during the time of the retreat—but maybe longer.

LORAINE
That's too good to be true.

TEDDY
You don't think I could do it, do you?

LORAINE
Oh, honey, I know you could do it. When you make up your mind to do somethin', you do it. You've got a will of iron. I only wish a little of that could rub off on me.

MICHAEL
Will you, Daddy?

TEDDY
We'll see. We'll see.
    [*Looking back at the house through the binoculars*]
Sure is a snazzy layout—don't you think?

LORAINE
Uh-huh.

TEDDY

I think it's a dilly!

LORAINE

[*Looking in the opposite direction*]
I just can't get over it bein' gone. Poor Clayton . . .
[*Lights fade on* LORAINE *and* TEDDY. *The spot stays on*
MICHAEL, *looking back and forth from* TEDDY *to* LORAINE,
from LORAINE *to* TEDDY, *almost as if he were watching a
tennis match, as sound of surf comes up . . .*]

Scene 4

MICHAEL *slowly crosses to the proscenium, where he exchanges the beach towel for two white turkish ones. He throws one over his shoulder and wraps the other around his waist, and then removes his boxer shorts. Over the above action* LORAINE *can be heard.*

LORAINE
[*Offstage*]
Michael! Ohh, Michael!

MICHAEL
[*Out front*]
Yessum!

LORAINE
[*Offstage*]
What's takin' you so long up there?

MICHAEL
[*Out front*]
I'm taking a bath.

LORAINE
[*Offstage*]
Your supper's ready.

MICHAEL
What'd Willy leave on the stove?

LORAINE
[*Offstage*]
Nothin' but good will. *I* am the chef tonight!

MICHAEL
[*Incredulous but delighted*]
You cooked?—What'd you fix?

LORAINE
[*Offstage*]
It's *suppose* to be a surprise! Now stop that dawdlin' and come on! You could have taken ten baths as long as you've been up there. And with as much water as you always put in that tub!

MICHAEL
You need a lot of water to take a bubble bath.

LORAINE
[*Offstage*]
Bubble bath! Honestly, Michael, you should have been a girl.
[LORAINE *enters to catch* MICHAEL *in a pose—perhaps wrapping his head in a towel as if it were a nun's wimple, dipping his fingers into the washbasin as if it were a holy-water font, making a pious sign of the cross before his mirror*]

MICHAEL
[*With a start*]
Ohhh!

LORAINE
[*Surprised as well*]
What's the matter?!

MICHAEL
You scared me!

LORAINE

Whatcha scared of—your shadow?

MICHAEL

You might as well *be* my shadow. Why don't you knock?

LORAINE

Why do I have to knock? I'm your mother. Now let me see behind your ears.

MICHAEL

Don't pull 'em!

LORAINE

I'm not gonna pull 'em.

MICHAEL

You do sometimes.

LORAINE

Only when you need it.
   [*She pushes him by the shoulders to sit down and investigates his ears. He grimaces*]
Just look!—there's a blackhead! Now let me get it!

MICHAEL

NO!

LORAINE

   [*Firmly*]
Michael, stop squirmin' and sit still. I'm not gonna have you with filthy ears!

MICHAEL
Well, do it fast!

LORAINE
I'm not gonna hurt you.

MICHAEL
You always say that.

LORAINE
[*Commanding*]
Hush!
[*She bends his head to one side and commences her excavation. He begins a low moan . . .*]

MICHAEL
Ooowwwwwww!

LORAINE
Whatcha yellin' about—it's all over!

MICHAEL
[*Rubbing his ear*]
You lied, you hurt!

LORAINE
Look at it! Big as a tick! Believe you me, you didn't have dirt in your ears as long as I bathed you in the tub with me.

MICHAEL
Well, don't get any ideas—we won't fit any more!

LORAINE
Ohh, my nails are just horrible!— Now let me see your little thing.

MICHAEL
No!

LORAINE
Come on, Michael, let me look at your talliwacker.

MICHAEL
No! I don't have any blackheads there.

LORAINE
Stop stallin' and let me look!

MICHAEL
Mama!

LORAINE
Michael. *You hear me.*

MICHAEL
    [*Defeated*]
Ohhh, *all right!*
    [*And he snaps his towel open upstage. She has a look and a poke*]

LORAINE
. . . Well . . . O.K.
    [*He glumly closes his towel*]
Now that wasn't so bad was it?
    [*Observing* MICHAEL *who is still drying himself*]
Now, put on your robe this instant—I don't want you catchin' cold. And hurry up about it!
    [*She exits and quickly goes downstairs. He pulls on his robe, steps into his slippers, and follows her down to the kitchen*]

MICHAEL
[*En route*]
Can I listen to Lux Presents Hollywood tonight?

LORAINE
Not until you do your lessons.
[*He enters the kitchen*]
Go sit down and put your napkin in your lap.

MICHAEL
What's the menu on this special occasion?

LORAINE
[*Serving him*]
Peas and okra—stop playin' with the silver—fried corn, smoth-
ered steak, sliced tomatoes! How's that suit your apparatus?
[*He smiles broadly for the first time*]
What're you grinnin' at? Huh? Sweet thing. Who do you love?
[*She bends and kisses him. He giggles*]
Silly willy!
[*She goes for a bowl, returns holding it with pads*]
Watch out for this one—hot, hot, hot. Stop singin' at the table!
Honestly, Michael, everyone always tells me what lovely table
manners you have, but God knows, one would never know it
when you're at home!

MICHAEL
[*Through a mouthful of food*]
Mama, please . . .

LORAINE
And don't talk with your mouth full. How is it?

MICHAEL
[*Through clenched teeth*]
Mmmmmmmmmmmmmm.

LORAINE

I think I'll tidy up here. I just can't stand things out of place.

MICHAEL

Aren't you gonna eat any supper?

LORAINE

Oh, honey, I couldn't eat a mouthful right now. I just can't cook food and smell it and have any appetite left. By the time you've finished foolin' with it, it makes you sick at your stomach to look at it— Why aren't you eatin' your good supper?

MICHAEL

I'm full.

LORAINE

    [*Incredulous*]

Whaaat? Michael, all I ever hear is "Why don't we ever have meals like other people?" And when I *do* cook, you won't eat.

MICHAEL

Why don't we ever eat together?

LORAINE

Well, you know why . . . your daddy's at work. He has to work to keep this terra-cotta tile roof over our heads. And I . . . Well, I just told you, I'd be sick if I tried to eat right now.

    [*Pause. She sees the look on his face*]

Ohhh, I know what you mean. But I gave up a long time ago, tryin' to get this family together for a meal. And if we ever *do*, you know how it ends up.

MICHAEL

Excuse me.

    [*Pointedly polite, he gets up from the table and goes upstairs*]

LORAINE

Where're you goin'?

[*Blankly staring at the food*]

Looks like I cooked it just so I could throw it out. —What're you doin' up there?

MICHAEL

Turning on the radio. The program goes on in a minute.

LORAINE

[*Clearing away the table*]

You haven't done your lessons yet. You heard what I told you!

MICHAEL

I don't have any homework. The sisters never give any the first week.

LORAINE

Well, the summer is over. We are not on the coast now. You know what that means. You know your daddy's rules—no picture shows except only on Friday and Saturday, and no radio until after you do your lessons.

MICHAEL

What time is he coming home?

LORAINE

How would I know.

MICHAEL

[*Finding the radio station*]

Hurry up! It's just about to start!

LORAINE
[*Excited*]
I'm comin'! I'm comin'! Get out my negligee and the nail-polish remover and my emery boards.
[*There are muffled sounds from the radio as he adjusts it. Then he retrieves the manicure articles. She continues talking as if he were still in the room, during which she opens a bottle of beer*]
I think I'll just work on myself tonight. Give myself a manicure, shampoo my hair. Roll it, set it, pluck my eyebrows, and try to get myself lookin' like a halfway-decent human bein' for Mass Sunday. What story's on tonight?

MICHAEL
Rebecca—hurry up!
[*She starts up the stairs with the beer and two glasses*]

LORAINE
Oh, that was a grand picture—Laurence Olivier and Jo Ann Fontaine.

MICHAEL
Joan Fontaine.

LORAINE
She's Olivia de Havilland's sister. They were born in China, you know.

RADIO VOICE
[*Following fanfare*]
Lux Presents Hollywood!

LORAINE
[*Enters bedroom*]
Boy! Put your feet under that cover!

[*He does. She hands him a glass and pours hers full; he unzips her dress for her*]
You're just bound and determined to get the croup, aren't you?
[*She slips out of her housedress and into her negligee as* MICHAEL *stares at her, filing his nails*]

MICHAEL

I don't have croup any more. I have asthma.

LORAINE

Well, asthma then.

MICHAEL

[*Extending his glass*]
Just a tap, thank you.

LORAINE

[*Pouring* MICHAEL *beer. Studying her glass of beer*]
I don't really like beer. Beer just goes through me like Sherman went through Georgia.
[*And she has a big swallow*]

MICHAEL

Shhhhh!!!

RADIO VOICE

And now, Daphne du Maurier's *Rebecca.*

LORAINE

[*Sits on bed, hugs* MICHAEL]
Are you warm enough?

MICHAEL

[*Smiles*]
Um-hum. Warm as toast.

LORAINE

It's still the best bed in the world.

[*She snuggles closer as the lights dim, leaving only* MICHAEL *in a spot. The* RADIO VOICE *begins. A pause, and he gets out of bed and moves to his own room as the narration finishes*]

RADIO VOICE

"Last night I dreamt I went to Manderley again. It seemed to me I stood by the iron gate leading to the drive, but the way was barred to me by a padlock and chain. I called to the lodge keeper but, peering closer through the rusted spokes of the gate, I saw that the lodge was uninhabited."

Scene 5

Lights come up full on TEDDY *in the kitchen and* LORAINE *in her bed.* MICHAEL *is visible in his room, eavesdropping as he dresses.*

TEDDY

Get your ass down here now and answer me.
[*Pouring a drink*]

LORAINE

Please, Teddy, I've got cramps pretty severe and I'm on edge and I want to stay on the bed.

TEDDY

You've always got cramps or a headache or you're down in your back or some damn thing when I want you to account for something.

LORAINE

[*Taking pills from a bottle by her bed*]
Look, I'm nervous as hell and I don't feel like arguin'.

TEDDY

Are you nervous because you've got something to hide?

LORAINE

I most certainly am not! I'm late and I'm afraid when I do start I'll start floodin' again! And if that keeps up, I'll have to have another operation.

TEDDY

Yeah, so LaSalle can have another Cadillac.

LORAINE

I wouldn't be alive today without that man.

TEDDY

Alive so you can live it up on the sly.

LORAINE

Leave me alone, please.

TEDDY

I said, Get your ass down here.
   [LORAINE *gets out of her bed and slowly comes downstairs*]

LORAINE

Anyone else drinks on the job, you fire them.

TEDDY

It's my place of business—I can do as I damn well please—and while I'm workin' at night, you go out! And you take Michael with you and pick up your friends.

LORAINE

I do not. I don't have any friends to speak of. I don't want any friends.

TEDDY

Well, then where are you while I'm at work?

LORAINE

Right here in this house! Alone with my child. Night after night, except on the weekends when Michael and I go for rides—or window shoppin'! I'd take an oath.

TEDDY

You act like I never take you anywhere.

LORAINE

[*Getting a glass of water and taking a pill*]
I didn't say that, Teddy.

TEDDY

We go to the coast.

LORAINE

Yes, and I love it when we do . . .

TEDDY

I took you to the World Series last year, didn't I?

LORAINE

The less said about that, the better.

TEDDY

You're just guilty about the way you acted.

LORAINE

The way *I* acted!

TEDDY

The same damn way you've always acted in front of other men.

LORAINE

That's not fair to say that of me! Because it's not true!
[MICHAEL *has come into view a few speeches back, edging
his way down the stairs, listening to this exchange. He is now
wearing his shirt and trousers*]

MICHAEL
[*Entering*]
What are you two arguing about?

LORAINE
Go back upstairs, honey.

MICHAEL
I can hear you upstairs.

TEDDY
Do what your mother said!

LORAINE
I can't help it if men look at me!

TEDDY
You don't have to look back! You don't have to *smile* back!

LORAINE
If they smile at me, I do. I'm flattered.

TEDDY
You're just like your sister!

LORAINE
No, I'm not!

MICHAEL
Please. Please, don't fight.

LORAINE
I have never been man-crazy in my life!

TEDDY

It's no news to anybody that I'm not keen on my brother-in-law —in fact, I despise his guts. But sometimes I feel sorry for the poor son-of-a-bitch because you pair of heathens make such a sucker out of him.

LORAINE

He's not all that easy to live with—fogy as hell.

TEDDY

She put her ass in a butter tub is what she did. If we don't go to the Sugar Bowl, I am not having those barbarians in this house at Christmas time!

LORAINE

Well, they're comin'! It's already been settled.

TEDDY

If I so much as see that goddamn black Buick in the driveway, I'm gonna get the pistol out of the safe and blow their fucking heathen heads off!

LORAINE

You'll have to kill me first!

TEDDY

With pleasure! You'll be target practice!

MICHAEL

Daddy!

LORAINE

It won't be the first time. There's already one bullet hole in my bedroom to prove what a mean and crazy bastard you are!

MICHAEL
Mama!

TEDDY
I will not subject myself to that bitch taking over around here.
I will not sit still and watch you slobber all over the old man.

MICHAEL
I like Aunt Hattiebeth.

TEDDY
Oh sure. Oh sure.

MICHAEL
And I like going to visit them during vacation.

TEDDY
Because they let you run hog-wild! Feed you chocolate candy
till you start gasping for breath or puke all over the place. Not
to mention letting you hang around roadhouse honky-tonks
all night playing the jukebox while they tank up!

LORAINE
Look who's talkin'!

TEDDY
I don't want him with people who have no concern for his
spiritual welfare.

LORAINE
Hattiebeth always makes him go to Mass on Sunday when
he's up there visitin'— He is the one who doesn't want to go
and who talks her into lettin' him skip it!

TEDDY

You'd let him stay in bed too if I didn't stand over you like some wild-animal trainer in the circus! You only agreed to be married by a priest to shut me up. You don't believe in anything!

LORAINE

What do you know about what I think or feel? Just because I'm not a fanatic like you!—in the front pew every time the bell rings! One thing I'll say for my sister and brother-in-law, at least *my* relatives never molested your son!

TEDDY
        [*Lunges at her*]
Don't you dare throw that up in my face!

MICHAEL
        [*Running between them*]
NO! No! Keep away from her!

TEDDY
        [*Trying to push him aside*]
Get out of the way!

LORAINE

Go ahead, beat me to a pulp! Set some good example!

MICHAEL

Mama, please . . .

TEDDY
        [*To* LORAINE]
You shut up!

MICHAEL
Both of you, please! Stop it!

LORAINE
    [*To* MICHAEL *as* TEDDY *goes to retrieve a bottle and a glass,*
    and pours himself a drink]
You asked me about those photographs taken at the Stork Club
and at Leon and Eddie's—why I had taken a razor blade and
cut out my face. Well, I'll tell you. Because my eyes were so
blacked and my cheeks so swollen you wouldn't have known it
was your mother!

TEDDY
    [*Taking a gulp of his drink*]
You slut.

LORAINE
You got me mixed up with some of *your* friends.

TEDDY
You shut up!

LORAINE
Don't you accuse me of anything after the mornings you've
stumbled in dead drunk after having holed up with God knows
who—so soused you didn't even know you were wearin' a pair
of satin bedroom mules!
    [TEDDY *throws the drink in her face*]

MICHAEL
DADDY!
    [*And* MICHAEL *rushes to* LORAINE]

LORAINE
It's all right. It's all right.

MICHAEL

Oh, Mama, Mama . . . here . . . sit down. Sit down and let me dry your face.

[*He grabs a dishcloth and starts to gently blot her tears and the drink from her face*]

. . . Don't cry. Mama, shhh, don't . . . don't cry.

[TEDDY *silently watches for a second, then turns, weaves unsteadily away and out of sight*]

LORAINE

Oh, *I'm* all right. He didn't hurt *you*, did he?

MICHAEL

No.

LORAINE

[*Drying her eyes, getting up*]

Well, come on, we're gonna pack our things and get out of here.

MICHAEL

We are?

LORAINE

I'm just afraid of him when he's like this.

MICHAEL

—I was hoping you'd say we'd leave! This time, let's never come back.

LORAINE

What do you mean?

MICHAEL

If you got a divorce, then we'd never have to come back! Then

we could move away together somewhere. To a city— Say yes.
Oh please, say yes.

LORAINE

Oh, Michael. I don't know about any of that right now. I just
want to get away from here before he has any more and starts
in on me again.

MICHAEL

Then where will we go? To Aunt Hattie's?

LORAINE

No. I don't want to go there. A little of her goes a long ways.
I don't feel well and I've got to take a little somethin' for it
and be quiet for a while.

MICHAEL

I wish I could drive. I wish I could drive us far, far away.

LORAINE

We'll go out on the edge of town and find some little motor
court for the night. And tomorrow or the next day he'll be
himself again and then we can come back.

MICHAEL

But I don't want for us to come back.

[*Pause*]

LORAINE
[*Quite calmly and directly*]
Michael—he's your father. And you know I've always tried to
teach you to love him, no matter what he's done. He means

well. And he tries. I will just have to try a little harder too. But I want you to respect him—I mean that. Because, after all, he is your father.

> [MICHAEL *is silent*]

Now come and help me pack.

> [*Lights fade, leaving only* MICHAEL *illuminated by the follow spot. He slowly crosses to the proscenium to retrieve his raincoat, a Kotex box wrapped in plain brown paper, and a pharmacy bag. Throughout this action* LORAINE *can be heard emitting a faint moan . . .*]

Scene 6

Lights come up on LORAINE *in bed.*

LORAINE
Darlin', is that you?

MICHAEL
[*Entering*]
Yes ma'am.

LORAINE
Did you bring the Demerol?

MICHAEL
Yes ma'am.

LORAINE
. . . and the Kotex?

MICHAEL
Yes.

LORAINE
Did you have enough money?

MICHAEL
I charged it. How do you feel?

LORAINE

[*Anxiously taking the bag from him, removing a pharmacy bottle*]

I'll be O.K. just as soon as this medicine takes effect.

[MICHAEL *gets a spoon from the bed table, kneels on the mattress beside her*]

Oh, honey, don't shake the bed! Just the slightest touch is like a knife goin' through my brain.

MICHAEL

[*Taking the bottle from her, rising*]

I'm sorry.

LORAINE

Don't spill it! Don't spill it!

[MICHAEL *carefully pours out a spoonful; she opens her mouth and he gives it to her*]

I thank you.

[*He replaces the cap on the bottle and moves toward the bathroom*]

And, baby, pick up your feet. Please, tiptoe. Tiptoe.

MICHAEL

I'm sorry. I'll put this in the medicine cabinet.

LORAINE

No. —Just leave it here by my bed.

[*He returns the bottle and spoon to her bedside table*]

Have you got many lessons?

MICHAEL

I did them at recess.

LORAINE

—Whatcha starin' at?

MICHAEL

I think I'll go out in the yard for a while.
[*He tiptoes into* TEDDY's *room to get the binoculars*]

LORAINE

Well, be sure and button up. And don't run.

MICHAEL

I never run. The boys down the street are playing basketball and I just want to watch them through the binoculars.

LORAINE

Willy left your supper on the stove whenever you're hungry.

MICHAEL

I'm not hungry.

LORAINE

You didn't buy any chocolate at the drugstore and spoil your appetite, did you?

MICHAEL

You know I'd get asthma if I did that.

LORAINE

—Thank you for stoppin' by Dr. LaSalle's to pick up the prescription.

MICHAEL

You're welcome.
[*Over this action, there is a distant, prolonged train whistle*]

LORAINE

Listen at that train. It makes me want to travel. I wonder where it's headed.

MICHAEL

No telling.

> [*He tiptoes out— She continues the weak, rhythmic moan. He comes down the stairs and walks slowly out to the apron of the stage. Kneeling, clasping his hands together and looking up*]

Dear God, I want to make a deal with you. Please don't punish my mama for my sins. I'm sorry for offending you—and I promise you that if you let her get well, I won't commit any more acts of self-abuse. No matter how strong the temptation. So please, let me have wet dreams and I'll keep my end of the bargain if you'll keep yours.

> [*And then he takes a Tootsie Roll out of his raincoat pocket, tears off the wrapper, and starts to eat it as he raises the binoculars to his eyes. The light on* LORAINE *fades out, but the spot holds on* MICHAEL . . .]

Scene 7

Thunder. TEDDY *lights a candle to reveal basement stairs.*
Sound of rain is heard. MICHAEL *runs to* TEDDY's *protective*
arms and they huddle tightly every time there is a roll of
thunder.

TEDDY

. . . And stay away from water and never turn on a light
switch with a wet hand.

MICHAEL

Yes sir.
> [*Pause. A thunderclap. It subsides.* MICHAEL *is now seated a*
> *step or two below so that* TEDDY's *knees form a kind of arm-*
> *chair*]

I wish we could fix it up down here.

TEDDY

You and your mama can think of more ways to spend money.

MICHAEL

To have a place where I could bring some people and we could
dance. It's comfortable and cozy down here.

TEDDY

That's because it is what it is—a cozy cellar. If you fix it all up,
it would be like the rest of the house. A little more concentra-
tion in the area of your studies and a little less time spent on
becoming the local Fred Astaire might not be a bad idea.

MICHAEL

You're not gonna yell at me any more, are you?

TEDDY

I'm through yelling. I'm now going to give you a quiet ul-
timatum. If you don't bring your marks up by next term, every
privilege gets taken away. If you only knew how many people
in this world don't have the opportunity . . .

MICHAEL

I know. I know all about it.

TEDDY

Well, if you know so much, why the hell don't you do something about it!

MICHAEL

Don't yell at me. That doesn't do any good. It just makes it
worse—like the time I misspelled the word on the card of
your Christmas present. All it did was make me sick.

TEDDY

I'll never get over that. How could anybody spell a simple
word like "from" with an e! "To Daddy, *frome* your son!"
   [*He pronounces the word "frommy." There is a clap of
   thunder.* MICHAEL *makes a dive back into* TEDDY's *arms.*
   TEDDY *holds on to him and ducks his head. Then, after it has
   passed, slowly looks up*]
. . . Mainly you shouldn't be around trees. When it rains a lot
of people run and stand under a tree. Well, there's nowhere
more dangerous to be when lightning strikes. So remember—
stay away from trees.

MICHAEL

Yes sir.
   [MICHAEL *gets up again, takes a few steps in a different*

direction. He stops, picks up an old, partially deflated basket-
ball, tries to bounce it. Dust billows out as it plops to the floor
and softly rolls away]

TEDDY

I was sure happy when you asked me to buy that. Of course I
never disapproved of your having dolls. But I can't deny, when
you asked for a basketball I was really thrilled. Not to mention
that I nearly fell over in the toy store.

MICHAEL

I wanted to learn how to catch. I hate it when people throw
things at me and expect me to catch them—like books and key
rings . . . and basketballs.

TEDDY

I can't understand it. You've got good coordination and timing
—you can dance. You should be able to find some rewarding
athletic outlet. I don't mean football, of course. But . . . *pos-*
sibly . . . basketball. Tennis surely. Or golf—which has always
looked boring as hell to me, but you might like it.

MICHAEL

I'd get asthma if I tried any of those things. You know that!

TEDDY

Maybe you'd overcome it by doing them.

MICHAEL

Maybe if we lived up north I could learn to ski. Skiing re-
quires coordination and timing but there's no exertion required.
All you have to do is stand there and slide down the hill.

TEDDY

I'm sure there must be more to it than that. If there isn't, that sounds boring as hell too.

> [*Another roll of thunder.* MICHAEL *runs back to* TEDDY *and they huddle together until it dies away. A door opens at the top of the stairs, spilling a shaft of light on* TEDDY *and* MICHAEL *as* LORAINE *is revealed, wearing a negligee. She never comes down the steps toward them but remains above them throughout her appearance*]

MICHAEL

> [*Holding up his arms defensively toward her*]

Shut the door!

LORAINE

> [*Amused*]

Well, if you two aren't a couple of screwballs!

TEDDY

Ohhhh, Jesus.

LORAINE

I felt like I needed a good laugh so I thought I'd come down and take a look at you two chicken-hearted coo-coos.

MICHAEL

Shut the door because of the draft!

LORAINE

I always know where to find y'all when it's rainin'.

MICHAEL

Drafts attract lightning!

LORAINE

Now who told you that, as if I don't know.

TEDDY
I didn't tell him that. He told *me!*

LORAINE
What are y'all talkin' about?

MICHAEL
Nothing.

LORAINE
Are you talkin' about me?

TEDDY
No, we're not talking about you!

LORAINE
Well, what *are* you talkin' about?

TEDDY
We were talking about your son's rotten, stinking grades.

LORAINE
Y'all are not fightin', are you?

TEDDY
Not yet.

LORAINE
   [*To* MICHAEL]
What's the matter, honey? Did you get a bad report card?

MICHAEL
Well . . . not as good as they have been.

TEDDY
It was a thoroughly disgusting stinkeroo.

LORAINE
What could be causin' this?

MICHAEL
I don't know.

LORAINE
I used to be able to help you with your lessons when you were smaller. I used to drill you and drill you on your catechism. You didn't fail your catechism, did you?

MICHAEL
It's called religion now. I failed math.

LORAINE
Arithmetic?

TEDDY
He better not have failed religion or you really would hear some yelling around here.

LORAINE
[All clear to her now]
Oh well. I never could help you on arithmetic. Although I did drill you on the multiplication table.

MICHAEL
I still don't know the twelves.

LORAINE
Well, honey, who does?

TEDDY

You taught him to count on his fingers which is positively the
wrong way to even begin to go about it!

LORAINE

Well, you're *teachin'* him to be afraid of lightnin'! Which is
positively crackpot!

MICHAEL

Will you please shut the door.

TEDDY

On your way *out!*

LORAINE

Lightnin' can't hurt you, honey. Why, I used to love to play in
the rain when I was a child—couldn't wait for it to pour down
so I could get wringin' wet!—or make paper boats and watch
'em go sailin' down the gutter and get swallowed up by the
sewer! Of course, once Eldred Barlow was swingin' on a limb
when lightnin' struck the tree, and he was split in half and
burned to a crisp.

TEDDY

What did I tell you about trees?

LORAINE

But that was a freak accident! Freak accidents happen all the
time—not just when it's rainin'. You ought to just gimme your
hand right this very minute and let's march outside together
and just stand there and say, *I am not afraid!*

MICHAEL

No!

TEDDY

Defy the elements! That's the rule of thumb you apply to everything!

[*Thunder and lightning.* MICHAEL *and* TEDDY *huddle*]

LORAINE

Rain is so relaxin'. I love to sleep in rainy weather. I think I'll get back on the bed right now and try and relax a bit. Excuse me.

[*And she moves out of sight, leaving the door ajar. Pause*]

TEDDY

I don't suppose she's told you, but I'm going to have to take her to Memphis to a hospital.

MICHAEL

Why Memphis?

TEDDY

It's a private place. It's been highly recommended by Dr. LaSalle.

MICHAEL

Why doesn't Dr. LaSalle treat her like he always has?

TEDDY

That old French-fried fart says it's beyond him now. Too many pills and shots for migraines and female trouble and nerves. She's hooked. And I'm going to have to take her to this hospital to get her off and back to where she can manage without being dependent on anything. Willy Mae can take care of you.

[LORAINE *is up in her bedroom by now and has begun to sing* "Red River Valley"]

MICHAEL
   [*Hearing her*]
She didn't shut the door.

TEDDY

The rain has stopped anyway. We can go out now.
   [LORAINE *continues to sing as* MICHAEL *blows out the candle.*
   Light fades from the scene but he alone remains encircled in
   the spotlight. He picks up his raincoat and removes a letter in
   an envelope from his pocket . . .]

MICHAEL
    [*Out front*]
Peabody Hotel, Memphis, Tennessee, Dear Son . . .
    [*A spot comes up on* TEDDY *on opposite side of stage*]

TEDDY
    [*Out front*]
Got a kick out of your note and I don't mean to be critical but
you spelled "towel" with two *l*'s and "pursue" p-*e*-r-s-u-e. Now
two misspelled words on one penny postcard is a bit strong to
my way of thinking, so I would appreciate it if you would get
the dictionary and check these out.
Mama is doing fine. All our fears seem to have been utterly
unfounded. I always suspected she might be a bit of a schizo,
but the doctors say she is as sane as sane can be. They also say
that she is uncooperative as hell, but this is my side of it.
I think you would like the Peabody. It has a very swanky
dining room—maitre d' and all—and right in the middle of the
lobby there's a fountain with a lily pond around it and real
live ducks quacking and paddling about. It's all a little rich
for my blood, but Mama wanted to stay here and I wanted to
do everything in my power to smooth things over and keep
peace before I had to admit her to the hospital. Memphis,
however, is one of the deadliest holes I've ever been caught
with my pants down in. I just can't understand it for a river
town. Absolutely no action. You practically have to go to the
Arkansas side to poop, and once you go, there's nothing but

a couple of buckets of blood laughingly called nightclubs, and one or two package stores. Man, I've really got the Beale Street Blues. So, as soon as I have another consultation with the head of the joint to find out how long she's going to have to stay to get straight, and pay the bill, I'm going to catch the Panama and leave this burg in the shade.

MICHAEL
    [*Out front*]
I. L. U. B. I. T. W.

TEDDY
    [*Out front*]
I love you best in the world.
    [*Light fades on* TEDDY. *Spot holds on* MICHAEL *as he puts on his raincoat and* . . .]

Scene 9

Marian Anderson begins to belt out "Ave Maria" at an ear-splitting volume. Lights come up to reveal TEDDY, *prone on the kitchen floor, passed out amid scattered phonograph records, snoring.* MICHAEL *crosses to look at* TEDDY *a moment, walks around him to turn off the portable phonograph, pick up and look at an empty gin bottle. He raps "shave-and-a-haircut" on the top of the cabinet, waits for a moment . . .*

MICHAEL
Hello? —Anybody home?
   [*Another snore from* TEDDY]
Oh. Out for the evening, as it were.
   [*Pause*]
Here, catch.
   [*And he tosses a set of keys on the floor*]
Thank you kindly for the use of your new car. It's a dilly!
   [*He heads for the stairs, starts to ascend them, stops, looks back, turns, walks back to stand over* TEDDY. MICHAEL *takes off his raincoat and spreads it over him, and goes up the stairs to his room to undress as* TEDDY *continues to snore, then gets up, gets his bearings, and heads for* MICHAEL's *room.* TEDDY *enters the room to find* MICHAEL *asleep. He sits on the edge of the bed, and picks up* MICHAEL's *hand. Pause*]
Daddy!

TEDDY
   [*Hushed*]
Yeah, it's only me. Shhhh . . .

MICHAEL
You scared me!

TEDDY
Oh. Sorry. Shhh . . .

MICHAEL
Why are you shushing? There's no one to wake up but me.

TEDDY
Oh. Forgot. Sorry. Can't seem to keep track of when the madame is "at home" or the madame is "at sea."

MICHAEL
What are you doing up?

TEDDY
Just holding your hand. Just listening to you breathe.

MICHAEL
I have to get up at five fifteen— I have to serve six o'clock Mass.

TEDDY
Oh, I'm so sorry I woke you up. Go back to sleep.

MICHAEL
O.K. Good night.
  [*He takes his hand from* TEDDY'*s, turns away*]

TEDDY
I'm sure proud of you. Serving Mass has always been a secret yen of mine. Maybe we could go by the church some time when it's empty and you could give me a few tips.

MICHAEL

It's a deal. Some time, but not now.
    [*He turns over again*]

TEDDY

What's that nice odor?—Kinda like lemons.

MICHAEL

It's some after-shave I bought.

TEDDY

    [*Reaching to touch him*]
I can't believe you have to shave already—your face is still
so smooth.

MICHAEL

That's because I shave. Twice a week.

TEDDY

    [*Laughs*]
I smell like oranges and you smell like lemons. All we need is
a couple of bells and we'd hit the jackpot!

MICHAEL

    [*Laughs, then stops*]
By the way, I didn't pay for it, I charged it.

TEDDY

    [*Stops laughing*]
Michael, you know I don't like that.

MICHAEL

I know, but I needed it and I had spent my allowance.

TEDDY
Son, you have to watch running up debts that you cannot pay. Your word *must* be your bond. *No compromising.*

MICHAEL
Yes sir.

TEDDY
[*Going right on*]
It's not that I don't want you to have luxuries. And the money's not important to me—it's the *principle.*

MICHAEL
Yes sir. I know.

TEDDY
Jesus once said, when someone criticized Mary Magdalene for using the perfume on his feet instead of giving the price of same to the poor—"The poor you will always have with you." So, he meant some things to be used for adornment. But he didn't say anything about charging them.

MICHAEL
Yes sir. I won't do it again.

TEDDY
Mary Magdalene, by the way, is one of my favorite saints. And one of Jesus' too. This is one of the most consoling lessons in the life of Christ—to love deeply the acknowledged sinner.

MICHAEL
Five fifteen is going to come awfully early.

[*Pause*]

TEDDY

Would it make you happy if I went on the wagon?

MICHAEL
[*Sitting up*]
What did you say?

TEDDY

I don't mean, take a pledge. I don't mean, swear before God in writing. But I will give you my word that, for a while, I'll dry out. At least till Mama gets home once again.

MICHAEL
[*Elated*]
Ohhhh, Daddy!
[*He throws his arms around* TEDDY *and hugs him*]

TEDDY

Now, you better get to sleep.
[TEDDY *lowers* MICHAEL *back onto his pillow and then kisses him on the forehead and tucks him in*]
Good night. I love you best in the world.

MICHAEL

I love you three.
[TEDDY *exits as lights dim to spot on* MICHAEL. *Pause.* MICHAEL *begins to get out of bed and put on his pants and shirt as . . .*]

Scene 10

A light comes up on LORAINE *in her room on the telephone.*

LORAINE
  [*Desperately and irately*]
. . . What do you mean, Dr. Dillon is not in his office—not
in his office to *me?* Is that what you mean! This is the thirty-
seven-thousandth time I've called in the past two days, so
you tell that bastard he'd better get on the line or I'm gonna
have the law on his tail for everything from sellin' morphine to
performin' abortions quicker'n he can say Booker T. Washington!
  [*Pause*]
Hello? . . . Hello!
  [*And she rapidly starts flashing the telephone bar as all the
  lights come up*]

MICHAEL
  [*Entering her bedroom*]
Dr. Dillon won't help you any more, Mama. He told you to
stop calling him.

LORAINE
  [*Putting down the phone*]
I wasn't callin' Dillion! I was tryin' to call your daddy.

MICHAEL
  [*Hopelessly shaking his head*]
Oh come on. You've been hiding from him all day yesterday

and today—pretending you're asleep when he leaves; pretending you're asleep when he comes in.

LORAINE
He's not comin' in early tonight, is he?

MICHAEL
Let's hope the hell not.

LORAINE
You think he knows?

MICHAEL
He knows it's just a matter of time.

LORAINE
I'm not goin' back to Memphis again! I've been in and out of that place too many times, and it just does no good! He's gonna have to try it *my way* for a change.

MICHAEL
You know he'll never go for that.

LORAINE
Maybe if you tried to convince him.
    [MICHAEL *doesn't answer*]
Well, what am I gonna do?

MICHAEL
I've tried to offer a solution.

LORAINE
Oh, Michael, that's so farfetched.

MICHAEL

You won't listen to *me,* just like he'll never listen to you. It's
a vicious circle.

LORAINE

Everything's a circle and it's all vicious. First, I'm overdue and
get one of those unbearable migraines, or else start floodin', or
both. And how long do you think any human bein' could
stand such pain without takin' something to kill it. The last
headache went on for eleven days before I finally gave in—and
then there's no turnin' back. And then, sooner or later, it runs
out. And here we are—right back where we were—not a c.c.
of anything left, not even a bottle of paregoric, and me goin'
into withdrawal like greased lightnin'! I tell you, when the
Lord put me together, I think it must have been from the
leftovers.

MICHAEL

   [*Quickly retrieves a slop jar from behind the bed*]
Are you going to be sick again?

LORAINE

No. But I better get back on the bed.
   [MICHAEL *helps her to lie down, covers her*]
Is it cold in here to you?

MICHAEL

No.

LORAINE

Oh. —How are things at St. Iggy's?

MICHAEL

Winding up slowly but surely. Boy, will I ever be glad to get
away from that bunch of meatheads.

LORAINE

I just can't feature your graduatin' and goin' off to college in the fall. Where has the time gone?

MICHAEL

It's seemed like forever to me.

LORAINE

That's because you're young. I was the same way when I was your age. Only I never finished high school. Hattiebeth did. But I never had the chance. I went to work when I was in the tenth grade as a switchboard operator.

MICHAEL

Aunt Hattie was the favorite, wasn't she?

LORAINE

That's puttin' it mild. After my pa died, my ma took everything we had and gave it to her. All I ever got was my ears boxed if I didn't chop enough wood or pump enough water from the cistern, while Hattiebeth stayed dressed up like a department-store dummy lookin' out the window at me work.

MICHAEL

Is that why you didn't go to Grandma's funeral?

LORAINE

I had a sick headache that day.—You know, I've often thought that might be one of the reasons I have these headaches—'cause my ma made me see stars so many times. I used to think it was from bleachin' my hair—that the peroxide seeped right straight through to my brain. And, of course, I never had anything to take for them. I'd just crawl up to the edge of the back

porch and let my head hang over the side and vomit and vomit.
Nobody ever bothered me. Nobody even knew I was there.

[*Pause*]

MICHAEL
Are you all right?

LORAINE
Oh, darlin', I wish I could answer yes, but I'm beginnin' to
shake to pieces.

MICHAEL
[*Insistent but encouraging*]
Mama, please, instead of thinking of ways of trying to get more
stuff—and since you don't want to have to go any place again
—let's do it here; go through it together. Right now, before
Daddy gets home.

LORAINE
Oh, darlin'!

MICHAEL
How long does it take?

LORAINE
You don't understand what it's like.

MICHAEL
Yes, I do. It won't scare me.

LORAINE
No. It takes time. I'd lose control. You couldn't manage me.

MICHAEL
Please, Mama, trust me.

LORAINE

Oh, I do trust you. But it's dangerous. I won't be able to stand it. I can tell that now. I'm chilled.

MICHAEL

I'll fill the tub up with hot, hot water—it'll relax you.
  [*He dashes offstage into the bathroom*]

LORAINE

What if I went into convulsions and your daddy caught us!
  [*The sound of running water begins.* MICHAEL *reappears . . .*]
. . . I can't. It's no use.

MICHAEL

Please. Please try. It'll be the answer to everything. You won't have to go anywhere and Daddy will never have to know. I'm sure we can do it together. Now, come on!

LORAINE

No! No, darlin', don't try to pick me up. I'm too heavy for you.

MICHAEL

No, you're not.

LORAINE

You'll hurt yourself.

MICHAEL

No, I won't.
  [*He pulls her to a sitting position on the bed*]

LORAINE

Oh, I'm cold. I'm so cold!

MICHAEL

The water will warm you up and relax you too. Come on!

LORAINE
[*With a touch of panic*]
Oh, Michael . . . honey . . . what am I gonna do?

MICHAEL
Please, Mama. Let me help you!

LORAINE
[*Unsteadily approaching him*]
O.K.—O.K.—whatever you say.

MICHAEL
Come on, now. Please, come on!

LORAINE
[*Near the bathroom entrance*]
. . . My nightgown.
[*She tries to pull the straps down over her arms*]
. . . I can't get it off.

MICHAEL
Never mind. Just get in the tub with it on. I'll find the scissors
and cut it off you after you relax. Now . . . please, please . . .

LORAINE
I'm comin'! I am.
[MICHAEL *helps her out.* TEDDY *enters the kitchen. He has a
paper bag with him. He climbs the stairs to his room, retrieves a glass, removes a half-empty fifth of gin, and pours
himself a drink. He is drunk but with a lucidity that alcohol
produces when it removes inhibitions—He is in an articulate
but violent rage. The following dialogue is offstage*]

MICHAEL'S VOICE
Now, be careful. Don't slip. Don't slip.
[*There is the sound of mild splashing and stirring of water*]

LORAINE'S VOICE
. . . Ohhhh . . . Ohhhh . . .

MICHAEL'S VOICE
Does that feel good?

LORAINE'S VOICE
. . . Yes . . . Ohhh yes . . .

MICHAEL'S VOICE
Is it too hot?

LORAINE'S VOICE
. . . Ohhhh! Michael! . . . I'm cold . . . I'm cold!

MICHAEL'S VOICE
I'll turn on the tap—let some more hot run . . .

LORAINE'S VOICE
No! It's too deep! I've got to get out! I've got to get out!

MICHAEL'S VOICE
Then grab me around the neck. That's right. Careful now . . .
careful.
[TEDDY *polishes off the drink, sets the bottle and glass down
in his bedroom*]

LORAINE'S VOICE
I've got to get back on the bed!

MICHAEL'S VOICE
Hang on! Hang on!
[TEDDY *enters* LORAINE's *bedroom just as* MICHAEL *appears,
carrying* LORAINE *in his arms. The ends of her hair and her*

*nightgown are thoroughly soaked, causing the fabric to be-
come partially transparent and to stick to her skin and reveal
her body.* MICHAEL's *shirt front and sleeves are wet*]

TEDDY

What the fuck do you think you're doing?

LORAINE

[*After a moment*]
Put me down, honey. I'm all right. I'm all right! Put me down
and get my bathrobe!
[MICHAEL *stands her up and rushes back into the bathroom*]
You've fallen off the wagon.

TEDDY

What did you fall off—a diving board?

LORAINE

No, dear. Just the deep end. I only fell off the deep end.
[MICHAEL *returns with a thick, full-length terry-cloth robe. He
assists her to put it on*]
Thank you, my angel.

TEDDY

A certain doctor came to see me today. It seems you owe him
a bit of a bill.

LORAINE

Teddy, don't fuss at me now. Please.
[*She ties the robe, moves to sit on the bed*]

TEDDY

Michael, I want to talk to your mother in private.

MICHAEL
[*Flatly*]
I already know about Dr. Dillon. I picked up one of the prescriptions and had it filled myself.

TEDDY
You *what?!*

MICHAEL
She needed it! She said it would be the last!

TEDDY
You fool! You punk!

LORAINE
Leave him alone, Teddy! I made him do it. So Dillon came by to collect in person. Well, I guess everybody and his sister Sue knows now.

TEDDY
I guess they do—'cause there we sat in my place of business for all to see—me and the biggest nigger doctor in town!

LORAINE
All right! So now you know. I get it when and where I can—behind your back, under your nose! Now maybe you'll listen to reason and try it my way!

TEDDY
Reason! What you're talking about don't make good sense!

LORAINE
It makes as much sense to me as whiskey does to you. I got along just fine until I couldn't get any more. If I stay in Memphis six weeks or six months, I shall always be as I am

now. I want and need a shot. Why not let's try it this way for once. Let me have a shot every four hours and I'll never try any way of gettin' any more. Let me live the rest of my life in as much peace as possible. I think this will be agreeable with Michael.

> [TEDDY *is silent.* MICHAEL *is silent.* LORAINE *turns to* MICHAEL . . .]

Tell him, Michael. Tell him it's all right with you.

MICHAEL
> [*Softly*]

It's . . . all right with me.

TEDDY
> [*Cynically*]

It's O.K. by you, is it?

MICHAEL

Maybe it would work.

LORAINE
> [*Trying to be firm, but really being desperate*]

I would like to know one way or the other as I'll try and make other plans.

TEDDY
> [*Mockingly*]

Oh, I see.

MICHAEL

We've tried everything else, it seems.

TEDDY
> [*Same attitude as before*]

I see. I see. I have to check with my adolescent son if it's O.K.

to supply you with dope—oh, but it's all right because he gives me his approval. And my wife, the dopehead, lays it on the line that if *I* do not *approve,* she will make other plans.

LORAINE

Now don't take it the wrong way. *Please.*

TEDDY
[*Heated*]
What's the right way to take it? And why should I take it at all!
[*To* MICHAEL]
I don't have to ask your permission for anything!
[*To* LORAINE]
And go ahead with your other plans. I'd like to know what they are. If you're gonna leave me—all right then, get out!
[*To* MICHAEL]
And you get out with her! You seem to prefer her company—to be in cahoots with her—so be it!
[*He goes back into his bedroom, takes the bottle of gin, starts to pour another one.* MICHAEL *quickly follows him, but keeps his distance*]

MICHAEL
[*Mock disbelief*]
You're not gonna take another drink!

TEDDY

I am. I most certainly am. And I don't need nor want your permission.

LORAINE

Michael, come away. Leave him alone.
[TEDDY *pushes past* MICHAEL, *going back to* LORAINE's *bedroom to confront* LORAINE *directly*]

TEDDY
[*Deliberate innuendo*]
And not *everything* has been tried!

LORAINE
You wouldn't let them give me those treatments! You promised you'd never let them do that to me!

TEDDY
You promised every trip to Memphis would be the last one!

LORAINE
The last one *was* the last one, as far as I'm concerned! I'm never goin' back there again.

TEDDY
You better believe it, you're not! Because I'm not throwing good money after bad. I'll be damned if I let you break me when you have no intention of changing!

LORAINE
That's right! As long as it is there to take, *I am goin' to take it!*

TEDDY
[*Grabs hold of her*]
I am going to have you committed! I'm going to have the shit shocked out of that crazy brain of yours!

LORAINE
[*Rushing to* MICHAEL]
NO! Michael! Michael, take me away from here!

TEDDY
And it won't be in some fancy joint either! I am going to have you put away in the state institution!

MICHAEL
[*Lashing out*]
You shut up! Don't you say those things to her!

TEDDY
[*Boiling*]
You just shut up your mouth, you impudent little shitass!

MICHAEL
You're the one who's crazy!

LORAINE
Michael!

TEDDY
What did you say to me?

MICHAEL
I said, you're the one who's crazy, you goddamn drunk!
[TEDDY *lunges at* MICHAEL]

LORAINE
TEDDY!

MICHAEL
[*Pulling away from him; fiercely*]
Get your goddamn paws off me, you drunken son-of-a-bitch!
[TEDDY *swings at* MICHAEL, *misses. But* MICHAEL *violently pushes him in the same direction he has swung, which causes* TEDDY *to fall to his knees. The moment he is down,* MICHAEL *rushes upon him, beating him with his fists*]

TEDDY
[*Bellowing drunkenly*]
Go on! Go on! Hit me! Hit me! HIT ME! HIT ME!
[*And he starts to laugh. Meanwhile,* LORAINE *runs between them, tries desperately to pull* MICHAEL *off* TEDDY]

LORAINE

Michael, stop it! *Stop it! He's your father!* HE'S YOUR
FATHER!

[TEDDY *stops laughing, grabs* LORAINE *by both her arms and
hurls her aside with such force that she is thrown to the floor.
She screams.* TEDDY *now subdues* MICHAEL's *arms, pulling
himself to his feet at the same time. The moment he is up, he
knocks* MICHAEL *back onto the landing.* LORAINE *screams
again*]

NO! NO! NOOOOOOOO!

[TEDDY *starts to come at* MICHAEL *again.* MICHAEL *backs into*
TEDDY's *room, grabs the gin bottle and cracks it over his skull,
smashing the bottle.* TEDDY *is genuinely physically stunned by
the impact—stops, staggers forward a step or two, loses
balance—one knee bends and he falls.* MICHAEL *is frozen with
fear.* LORAINE *is still crouched on the floor, whimpering. A
moment . . . a tick of the clock or a heartbeat when all are
breathlessly still. Then* TEDDY *grabs his head as blood begins to
stream down over his face.* LORAINE *sees it and covers her
mouth to suppress a still-audible, monotonous moan.* MICHAEL
remains immobile—transfixed. TEDDY *removes his hand from
his head, holds it before him to see his bloody palm*]

TEDDY

[*Incredulously; glazed look at* MICHAEL]

. . . You! . . . You've hurt me.

[*He loses his equilibrium and falls forward to catch himself
with his free arm*]

MICHAEL

[*With increasing volume*]

. . . Willy! *Willy Mae!* WILLY MAE!

[*And he bolts down the stairs, yelling*]

CALL AN AMBULANCE! CALL AN AMBULANCE!

[*He stops at the foot of the stairs, trembling visibly.* LORAINE
*has gotten to her feet, staggered to her bed where she col-
lapses sobbing . . .* TEDDY *has now crawled to the top of the
stairs,* MICHAEL *turns to see him*]

. . . Oh God, oh God, oh God, oh God, oh God . . .

[*And he starts to run—this direction, then that direction—then another, and another, until he bolts to the apron of the stage and doubles up on his knees sobbing . . . Lifts his head heavenward and screams through clenched teeth*]

. . . Oh God! Oh God— Goddamn you, God. You broke your end of the bargain! *GODDAMN YOU!*

BLACKOUT

ACT 2

Scene 1

A spot comes up on MICHAEL, *lying in his bed. Then lights come up to reveal* LORAINE *in her room. A brief pause, and she crosses toward* MICHAEL's *room. She is wearing a jersey negligee. The fabric clings to her curves and falls to the floor in soft flowing folds; however, she is dissipated, slightly disheveled, and ill.*

LORAINE

Darlin'? Can I come in?

MICHAEL
[*Tonelessly*]
—Sure.

LORAINE
[*Entering*]
It's so dark in here—don't you want me to open the Venetian blinds?

MICHAEL

No ma'am.

LORAINE

. . . Or turn on a lamp?

MICHAEL

No ma'am.

LORAINE

Or turn down the air conditioner—it's like the North Pole in
here.

MICHAEL

No. I like to listen to the hum.

LORAINE

Well, it's gonna rain this afternoon and cool off. Have you got
a headache?

MICHAEL

No. —How's yours?

LORAINE

Better. There's still a little throbbin' in one temple and I'm
weak as a kitten but I just need some rest.
    [*Picking up a box of candy by his bed*]
Chocolate bonbons! Where'd they come from?

MICHAEL

I bought them. Would you like one?

LORAINE

No thank you. —Kinda heavy. —Maybe that's what got you
feelin' bad.

MICHAEL

I eat chocolate all the time now.

LORAINE

No more asthma attacks?

MICHAEL

No.

LORAINE

Why, that's the best news I've had since Hector was a pup!
You must have outgrown it.

MICHAEL

I must have.

LORAINE

Well, don't eat too much of it or it'll make you sick anyway.

MICHAEL

I won't.
[*There is a roll of thunder*]

LORAINE

Ohhh! Just listen at that thunder!
[*Peeping out through the Venetian blinds*]
We are goin' to have an electrical storm. It is just as hot and
still as it can be. Clouds have covered the sun and the trees,
and the grass looks like green neon.
[*Turns back to* MICHAEL, *crosses slowly toward his bed*]
. . . Is that why you're lyin' here in the dark, honey? Are you
still scared of the lightnin'?

MICHAEL

No.

LORAINE

[*Sits on bed, takes his hand*]
Why, your little hand is like ice! Michael, you've got me
worried. All you've done this entire week is mope. Seems like

the only reason you came home from college was to deliver
your dirty laundry.

MICHAEL
    [*Distantly*]
Has it only been a week?

LORAINE
You remind me of some of those vegetables I've been locked
up with who do nothin' but stare into space.

MICHAEL
I just don't feel like getting up, that's all.

LORAINE
    [*Continuing to warm his hand*]
Do you miss Washington and your friends at school?

MICHAEL
Some of them.
    [*Another roll of thunder. She embraces him*]

LORAINE
—I know what's wrong with you—you need a girl. Come on,
now. Why don't you get up and call up some of your old
friends here. Maybe they'll take you out to the country club
for a swim. You like goin' out there, don't you?

MICHAEL
Not always as their guest.

LORAINE
Well, you know your daddy and I don't care a thing about
that crowd of social climbers. He would *never* join, but he has

always said he'll pay for your membership as soon as you're
old enough to be accepted on your own.

MICHAEL
I wouldn't go near any swimming pool with it so threatening
out.

LORAINE
—Well . . . why don't you give a party?

MICHAEL
When?

LORAINE
Tonight!

MICHAEL
A party—with you sick in bed?

LORAINE
Oh, honey, don't mind me—you're young! You've got to have
your friends!

[*Pause*]

MICHAEL
Wouldn't all the noise . . .

LORAINE
I won't hear a thing way upstairs in my room.

MICHAEL
But what about Daddy?

LORAINE

Oh, you know he won't care—he wants you to enjoy your summer vacation. Why don't you get on the phone right now and call everybody and say you've just decided to have a bash!

MICHAEL

I'd have to have something to serve them when they showed up.

LORAINE

Tell Willy to boil a pot of shrimp and fry some chickens and make a great big bowl of potato salad.

MICHAEL

Willy won't like the idea.

LORAINE

She ain't got nothin' to say about it. There's plenty of liquor in the house, and if you run out, there's plenty more where that came from!
> [*There is a flash of lightning, followed by a clap of thunder.* MICHAEL *flinches visibly, buries his face in the pillow. She puts her arms around him*]

Don't be such a scaredy-cat. No matter what Daddy says, lightnin' won't hurt you. It's really pretty. Look at it sometimes.
> [*No response*]

Move over and let me lie down. My headache is just killin' me.
> [*He slides over a bit and she gets under the covers with him, holding him in her arms. As the light dims on them, light comes up on* TEDDY, *glass in hand, slowly climbing the back stairs to his room. He picks up a pamphlet, settles on bed to read it while sipping his drink. A spot comes up on* MICHAEL, *tying his tie. A piano is playing some Cole Porter in the background.* MICHAEL *goes to the door, raps "shave-and-a-haircut" on it, then quietly enters*]

MICHAEL
[*Sotto voce*]
Daddy?

TEDDY
Hi. Whatcha doing up here?

MICHAEL
I'm just checking to see if you're home. I didn't hear you come in.

TEDDY
Been here about an hour. Took some of your ice from the kitchen and came up the back way. Didn't want to interrupt anything.

MICHAEL
You always say that. You wouldn't have interrupted anything. You should have come in for once and said hello to everyone.

TEDDY
Now, Michael, you know that's not my speed.

MICHAEL
Just to say hello?

TEDDY
Let's not argue about it, shall we?

MICHAEL
Why are we whispering?

TEDDY
Why did you tiptoe in? We're conditioned not to wake the sleeping beauty in the next room.

MICHAEL

If she can sleep through the music from downstairs, she's not going to hear us through a closed door.

TEDDY

I wouldn't take odds on it. Our whispers produce an effect on her eardrums not yet discovered by RCA Victor!

MICHAEL

What are you reading?

TEDDY

Some new religious literature I sent away for and the *What's On in Las Vegas* magazine.

MICHAEL

Well. What's on?
  [*Sits on bed beside* TEDDY *and lights cigarette*]

TEDDY

I haven't gotten there yet. I'm still stumbling through the desert with Thomas Aquinas.

MICHAEL

Sure you won't stumble downstairs with me for just a second?

TEDDY

Honey, don't put me on the spot. I'm all for you and I want you to be right along with the next one—but all that to do is just too strong for me. Let me enjoy my nip by myself.

MICHAEL

. . . Well . . . O.K. Please don't drink too much.

TEDDY

Don't worry about me getting swacked; just watch out for yourself.

MICHAEL

Do I seem high to you?

TEDDY

No. But you seem mellow as hell.

MICHAEL

Well, let's not argue about that, shall we?

TEDDY

I have nothing against your choice of friends—I mean the fact that they are quite a bit older than you—that doesn't matter. I always ran with an older crowd—it's a great way to learn the score. But they are adults and they can really put the sauce away—so don't you feel like you have to match 'em or you'll wind up on your ass.

[LORAINE *sweeps in, dressed to the nines—hair, jewelry, the* works]

LORAINE

I thought I heard you two in here.

TEDDY

Well now, looka here. I'd say you're dressed up enough to go to a party.

LORAINE

How do I look?

MICHAEL

Like you've recovered.

TEDDY

I thought you weren't feeling well today.

LORAINE

You know me, I can put up a good front. I felt like it wasn't fair to our son not to have one of his parents put in an appearance.

TEDDY
[*To* MICHAEL]
She doesn't want them to think that we're myths!
[*To* LORAINE]
Where'd you get the snazzy outfit?

LORAINE

I bought it ages ago. But it's still in style—simple things always are!
[*To* MICHAEL]
Why aren't you downstairs? What were you two talkin' about?

MICHAEL

Nothing.

LORAINE

Were y'all talkin' about me?

TEDDY

No, God, no, we weren't talking about you.

LORAINE
[*To* MICHAEL]
Well, you ought not to be away from your guests so long.

TEDDY

Then I guess it's left up to you to rectify the situation.

LORAINE

I'm only goin' to stay for a second. Just long enough to let everybody know you do have a mother.

TEDDY

There'll be little doubt of that by the time you leave.

LORAINE

Fortunately I *have* been blessed with the gift of gab. But you can just about win anybody over if you are warm and charmin'.
[*To* MICHAEL]
Don't you be long. I don't want them to think *you're* rude.

MICHAEL

I'll be right down.

LORAINE

[*Takes* MICHAEL'*s cigarette*]
Tell me who's here so I'll know what to expect.

MICHAEL

Oh, Mary Jo and Charleen and Jerome and the same old crew.

LORAINE

Charleen Cunningham! Why, she's got children as old as you!

MICHAEL

I don't like her children. I like her.

LORAINE

Well, wish me luck!
[*She exits the bedroom and sweeps down the stairs . . . Descending grandly*]

Why, Charleen, what a surprise to see you here! And Jerome! I haven't seen you since the Valkenberg-Ortega rites. Weren't they the most gorgeous corpses you've ever seen?

[*She exits as the lights dim, except for the spot which follows* MICHAEL *as he comes center. Pause. He goes to the proscenium* . . .]

Scene 2

. . . to get his raincoat and a valise. Lights come up full on TEDDY *in the living room. He is wearing pajamas and a dressing gown.* MICHAEL *enters the scene.*

MICHAEL

I still don't understand why you haven't written a word since you were in Washington. What's going on? Have you been on a tear ever since you got back—you were well on your way when you left.

TEDDY

I hope you have the Christmas spirit.
 [MICHAEL *sets down the valise, notices an oxygen tank on a dolly*]

MICHAEL
 [*Removing his raincoat*]
What's the lowdown on this attractive accessory for the home?

TEDDY

In case of emergency. The living room is now my bedroom. Stairways are not advised.

MICHAEL
What happened?

TEDDY

I'd been back from seeing about you for almost three weeks when I just ran down. The doctor said that digitalis wouldn't get my ticker back on the track and that I'd better check into the hospital. The following morning I had a spell, which was later diagnosed as angina pectoris. After the storm and treatment I was released and have been here ever since.

MICHAEL
I knew something was up.

TEDDY
That has absolutely nothing whatsoever to do with why I have not answered your letters.

MICHAEL
[Referring to the tank]
I guess one is not supposed to smoke around this thing.

TEDDY
Not unless you'd like us to personally attend Jesus' birthday party. We can go in the next room.

MICHAEL
Never mind. Don't keep me in suspense any longer.

TEDDY
It was impossible for me to write because I was terribly upset by the disrespect shown me, particularly the night I took you and your friend to supper. It's taken time for me to think it out and try to understand why I am always to blame.

MICHAEL
Has it ever occurred to you that you might start by considering your behavior?

TEDDY

Believe it or not, I was trying my damnedest to be on my *good* behavior. When I found out that your impacted tooth was nothing and that you'd already recovered, I thought we might celebrate and shoot the works.

MICHAEL

Well, you shot a little wide of the mark. Your behavior, if there can be any doubt in your mind, was insulting and embarrassing to me and to my friend.

TEDDY

A great deal of it could have been avoided by a little tact on your part.

MICHAEL

Why should I have to account for *your* conduct! You *are* an adult, aren't you?

TEDDY

You're damn right, I am. And I am your father too!

MICHAEL

So that's it. What you want is for *me* to apologize to *you.*

TEDDY

No matter what you believe, I did not come to Washington to get drunk. I can do that here. I did pretty well until that night.

MICHAEL

Yeah, and then you got smashed and made up for lost time. Made an ass of yourself in the restaurant and fell asleep in the theater. Snored so loudly that you had to be dragged back to the Willard and undressed and dumped into bed like a heap of garbage.

TEDDY

And you told me that you *hated* me!

MICHAEL

I *did!* And I've got a witness!

TEDDY

And that your mother and I had no love for you.

MICHAEL

You've got a keen memory even when you're fried!

TEDDY

Not such a very long while back, here in this very house, I heard you say to your mother that you wished she were dead. And now, in a hotel room in Washington, D.C., you tell me that you . . . hate me!

MICHAEL

Jeeeezuz, we haven't been together five minutes and . . .

TEDDY

Who held you when you were a baby and had the croup and couldn't breathe? Your mama used to sit up all night in a rocker with you on a pillow. You might not believe it, but I did get up occasionally to check on you. And when you were still frail, Mama would drive to St. Ignatius' Academy and feed you hot soup on the back seat. Several of these times your father was present.

MICHAEL

What do you want, a medal for not letting me suffocate or starve?

TEDDY

I insisted on your being an altar boy throughout school . . .

MICHAEL

That you certainly did.

TEDDY

Besides which, you had all the material things of life: toys, clothes, money, warm home, the use of a car at an early age, and either one or two idiots worrying about the time of night, watching every passing vehicle to see if it would turn safely into the driveway.

MICHAEL
   [*Boiling*]
I still say that if you really loved me so much, you wouldn't have tried to pay me off so, but would have tried to do something about your sorry state of affairs.

TEDDY

What your mother and I do to ourselves has got nothing to do with *you!*

MICHAEL

But it does! I am included whether you want me to be or not! All the three of us do is torture each other. You call this a home? A home to come home to? It's a nightmare!

TEDDY

I never wanted this place.

MICHAEL

I know! It was for *me*. Always for me.

TEDDY

Your mama wanted it too. And don't say you didn't.

MICHAEL

Of course I did. I was dumb enough to believe that if it looked legit from the outside, it must be legit inside!—How many times do you think I've watched that same street for hours wondering where the hell either of you were, and when you *did* show up, wondering if you could make it by the side of the house without taking off half the porch—which you have accomplished on occasion.

TEDDY

Since you were eleven years of age you seemed to have a contempt for me. I figured it would wear off with the years. But I see you now resent me more than ever. Certainly you know the only way to overcome this is to bring it out in the open. According to what you say, the trouble with me seems to be overdrinking. Is that really all?

MICHAEL

That's too cryptic for me. I'm afraid you'll have to bring that out in the open!

TEDDY

I remember once I was ashamed of your Aunt Maureen and our home in St. Louis because I ran with a better financial class of boys. We had neither electricity nor bath facilities, and your Aunt Maureen was dressed about fifteen years behind the times, and it made me feel backward.

MICHAEL

I am not exactly reluctant to invite my so-called "social-climbing" friends into this house. Everyone in this town knows exactly who we are—your place of business is on display on the busiest corner of the main drag.

TEDDY

Everyone in this town is a cornball and you know it!

MICHAEL

It is you who signs hotel registers with your occupation as "merchant."

TEDDY

It's a good word to cover a lot of things! Besides, that is what I am. A tobacco merchant. But I am not unaware for one minute that Connelly's Smoke House has nothin' to do with sausages. It's a pool hall. And there are punch boards and tips on the games and dominoes and a bar that serves liquor in a dry state and a lunch counter with one of the best short-order cooks this side of the penitentiary. But beyond that, it is a sports center, a fine one, like it says on the stationery, "Where All Good Fellows Meet." And you never need be ashamed of the Connelly background—my grandmother was a nun!

MICHAEL

What do you mean she was a nun?

TEDDY

A novice, that is, and she hightailed it over the wall to marry a brick contractor who was working in the convent. He was one of the best, mind you, laid every brick street in St. Louis.

MICHAEL

Among other things.

TEDDY

That friend of yours who was the witness to the debacle in the capital city—he was a nice boy, but I dare say he'd seen a drunk before in his life. And if he hadn't, it was an enlightening experience for him. What was his name?

MICHAEL

David Zimmerman.

TEDDY

Oh yes. Well, maybe he never *had* seen one before. I understand there's not a high rate of alcoholism at B'nai B'rith.
> [*He picks up a liquor bottle, looks at the bottle, shakes his head, looks back to* MICHAEL, *puts it down*]

I received a letter today from Mama telling me that she had convulsions and chewed up her tongue pretty bad.

MICHAEL

I don't care if she chewed it up, swallowed it, and digested it. At least I'd never have to listen to her again.

TEDDY

She had to have three blood transfusions—they had to cut into her arms to find the veins.

MICHAEL

I don't care if they had to amputate her arms—then *I'd* never have to get another letter from her.

TEDDY

> [*Incensed*]

She said to tell you she received her birthday gift and was most pleased. And to tell you that she is not able to write you.

MICHAEL

Able to write you, but not me.

TEDDY

I didn't think you wanted to hear from her!

MICHAEL

I don't want to hear that shit! That's all I've ever heard. Do you know how I dread getting a letter from her? I start shaking the moment I see the goddamn envelope. I break out in a cold sweat and get dizzy when I finally tear it open, and after I read it, I cry and throw up. If once, if only once, I could get a letter that wasn't a horror story! I am so goddamn sick of highballs and hypodermics, attempted suicides and oxygen tanks, remorse, self-delusions, broken promises, and, on top of it all, God, God, God. God, God!

TEDDY

Stop it! I can't take it!

MICHAEL

You can take it. If you can dish it out, you can take it. And if you can't, have a heart attack right here on the spot and let me watch. Yes, yes, yes, I said it before and I'll say it again, *I wish she were dead and I hate you and I hate her and I wish you were dead!*

TEDDY

GODDAMN YOU, YOU ARROGANT SNOB! I'm going to tell you the same as I told your mother the day you left home to go away to college. I said I had your entire education paid for and it was a tremendous pressure off of me and I was not going to be abused any more by anybody!

MICHAEL

ALL RIGHT THEN, GODDAMNIT. ALL RIGHT, YOU
WIN. I'M SORRY! If that's what you want to hear, then
Christ Jesus all right, I'M SORRY! PLEASE FORGIVE ME!
FORGIVE ME, FATHER. FORGIVE MY SINS. O.K.?—O.K.?
[*Sighs*]
No. I mean it. I do. I am sorry. I am. I am. And I guess I *am*
sorry that you aren't a doctor or a lawyer, but a cigar-store
Indian chief. And that she always behaved like Betty Grable
and Lana Turner, and never did what Claudette Colbert did,
or what Irene Dunne done.
[*Quiet. Pause*]

TEDDY

I hope you will not continue to profane God's name. That's
reducing yourself to my class.

MICHAEL

Do we *have* to drag God into this?

TEDDY

And I don't mean, by any measure, I expect you to be a goody-
goody. I have no time for them.

MICHAEL

You don't have to worry about that with me.

TEDDY

We do not know who is right or wrong. God will judge us all—
So I ask you . . . that as long as you live . . . don't ever try
to get even with anyone.
[*Lights dim on* TEDDY, *spot stays on* MICHAEL . . .]

Scene 3

. . . as he moves and sits down.

MICHAEL
[*Out front*]
Dear David . . . I think the main reason you and I never write to each other is because we feel that if we write we have to write well. I say to hell with that—so for better or worse, here goes. I miss you, you dumb Jew! How I wish I'd accepted your parents' invitation for the holidays. Here it's strictly the same song, second verse. The past few New Years seem only to have introduced a new illness or another operation. Consequently we've been skipping the Sugar Bowl jaunt and deluding ourselves that it's so much nicer to plan a real Christmas at home with just the three of us. This usually consists of my extravagant overdecoration of the house, only to have Loraine spend the day in the local clinic singing "Red River Valley," for me to eat dinner at someone else's home, and for Teddy to wind up blotto on the kitchen linoleum with "Ave Maria." Oh, how I wish I were with you, blotto on your living room rug, singing "Rio Rita"!
But again this year she broke down like clockwork around the end of November, so Teddy has revived the New Orleans gambit in an attempt, I suppose, to take the curse off things. He and I are about to leave now. But first we have to go visit her on our way.
The scenario goes like this: After you turn off Highway 80, just outside of Jackson, there is a short drive on a country road

before you reach Whitfield, Mississippi. And to anyone who's ever heard of it, that word in itself is synonymous with, and euphemistic for, insane asylum. Because, after all, that's what it is—primarily. But there are others who are not there on mental papers but who have been legally committed for alcoholism and narcotic addiction.

After you've ridden along the side road for a way, the first indication that you are nearing the place is the appearance of a long double row of tall shade trees on either side of the blacktop. It's one thing to me to drive beneath those welcoming trees in the summertime; whether it is taking her out there once again, or passing back through them after a visit, either way, coming or going, in summer that phalanx of green means *freedom*.

But always at this time of the year—or rather, at this time of day on this very same day of the year, the bare branches against the December light are never a thrilling indication that, at last, at least for a while, it is almost over. On this day, there is always a sense of disappointment that already we have arrived . . .

[*A spot comes up on* TEDDY, *holding a tray on which there are several brown paper bags covering various pots and pans*]

TEDDY
[*Out front*]
Give her the signal on the horn.

MICHAEL
There's no need to—there she is waving through that upstairs window.

[*A spot comes up on* LORAINE, *waving*]

TEDDY
[*Out front*]
Give it to her anyway.

MICHAEL
[*Out front*]
Daddy, it's a hospital.

TEDDY
[*Out front*]
Shit, it's Christmas too.
[*Car horn sounds "shave-and-a-haircut-two-bits" as* MICHAEL *rises and goes to the proscenium to collect a gift-wrapped package*]

LORAINE
[*Out front*]
Hurry up there! Hurry up with the key to this ward! Woman, you are as slow as Frankenstein walkin' through glue!

MICHAEL
[*Out front*]
My God, you can hear her even through a steel door. I sure would hate to be cooped up with her with nothing stronger than vitamin B-12.

TEDDY
[*Out front*]
She was a wonderful mother to you when you were young. She helped you when you couldn't help yourself. She can't help herself now. Be kind to her.
[*All the lights come up*]

LORAINE
Hey there!

MICHAEL
Hi.

TEDDY
Santy Claus!

LORAINE
     [*Rushing forward*]
Oh my goodness gracious! You both look just beautiful!
     [*They all embrace and kiss simultaneously*]
. . . Oh, look at that package! It's just wrapped grand!
     [*To* MICHAEL]
Did you do that, darlin'?

MICHAEL
Not this year. I had it done at the Special Wrapping Desk at
Julius Garfinckel's.

TEDDY
     [*Indicating the tray*]
And we got a sack!

LORAINE
Oh, and I bet I know what's in it.

TEDDY
Good old cornbread dressing that Willy Mae made. And giblet
gravy.

MICHAEL
And turkey . . .

TEDDY
And sweet potatoes with marshmallows on the top that Hattiebeth sent.

LORAINE

Well, you know I've never been one for sweets. But it all sounds delicious. Here, put these down a minute so I can get a good look at my husband and my child.

[*To* MICHAEL]

I guess I should say my son—you're a grown man, aren't you? But you'll always be my baby. I love your haircut—shaped so becomin'. And that's a gorgeous suit. Is it new?

MICHAEL

Uh-huh. I got it at the Georgetown Shop. It's Ivy League.

TEDDY

[*To* LORAINE]

The Ivy League sounds like the Big League, don't it?

LORAINE

[*To* TEDDY, *flirty*]

You look pretty Big League to me yourself.

TEDDY

[*Tongue-in-cheek*]

I still smell like orange juice.

LORAINE

[*Kissing him, nuzzling his check*]

Mmmmmmmmm. You sure do. And a little something else too.

TEDDY

[*Breaking away*]

Oh Lordy, here we go.

LORAINE

[*Defensively*]

Now, did I say something? I'll change the subject.

TEDDY

[*Directly*]

I told you, Mama, I took a pledge till Christmas Day and I have honored that pledge.

LORAINE

I know you've been good. Your word is as good as gold. I didn't mean anything. You look wonderful. You do.

TEDDY

And so do you.

LORAINE

[*Flattered, fishing for a compliment*]

Do I?

TEDDY

[*Sincerely*]

You sure do. You look just as pretty as the first day I ever saw you.

LORAINE

Well, I tried. I was so excited about seein' the two of you—I've been up half the night tryin' to decide what to wear—laid out my clothes a hundred times. It seems like no matter what I do to *myself*, I take such good care of my things—*they* just never wear out. I hope I don't look tired, do I? I'm not. Just nervous as a cat with a crocheted tail. Guess you can tell that though.

TEDDY

You seem fine.

MICHAEL

Yes. Just fine. You look marvelous.

LORAINE
It's just gonna take a little time, that's all.

MICHAEL
Sure.
[TEDDY *is silent.* LORAINE *senses this*]

LORAINE
What Mass did you go to?

MICHAEL
Eleven.

LORAINE
Did you both go to Communion?

MICHAEL
[*Flatly*]
Side by side.

LORAINE
Well, have you had anything to eat?

MICHAEL
I had a glass of water and then a piece of turkey.

TEDDY
I had a drink. —Just one. Just a little toddy to be somebody.

LORAINE
[*Exasperated*]
Oh, I declare, you two! A piece of turkey and a toddy!

TEDDY
We're savin' space for all that good rich food in Noo Awlens.

LORAINE
And all the bourbon on Bourbon Street.

TEDDY
Now, Mama, don't razz me.

LORAINE
What y'all got planned?

TEDDY
Same thing as always.

MICHAEL
Drive down by way of the coast so Daddy can stop at the monastery and see some of those priests who conduct those retreats.

TEDDY
Just to say hello and slip 'em a fin.

LORAINE
You can't buy your way into heaven, you know.

TEDDY
Don't have to. Heaven is my home.

LORAINE
And I know *you* in our old stompin' ground. —You'll have to stop at the Edgewater or Paradise Point . . .

TEDDY
[*Pleasurably and acknowledgingly*]
. . . and have one good jolt and some great seafood.

LORAINE
Well, all I ask is, please be careful.

TEDDY

I'm not going to be driving, *he* is.

LORAINE

I know he'll be drivin'—but not all the drunks on the highway
are behind the wheel. I mean, be careful about your health.
If you don't know it by now, you never will—that when you
lose your health nothin' else is worth very much.

TEDDY

That's right. If I don't know it by now . . .

MICHAEL

Please, let's not have a fight right here.

TEDDY

Who's fighting?

MICHAEL

We are about to.

LORAINE

That's another thing—I don't want you two fightin' on this trip!

MICHAEL

We never fight when there's just the two of us. —Well, not as
much.
    [*To* LORAINE]
Just like you and I don't fight when there's just the two of us.
And the two of you get along better without me.

TEDDY

I guess we don't work in three's as well as we do in two's.

LORAINE

Well then, since *I* won't be there, try to have a good time.

TEDDY

We *always* have a good time.

MICHAEL

Better every year. Really.

TEDDY

Careful what you say—she might not be in here when you get home next Christmas.

LORAINE

Oh, I'm not jealous of you two! It's just that when you talk about nice places and lovely things, it sure makes me want to be out of here. I wonder just how long I really will be here.

TEDDY

Well, if you would cooperate with the doctors for a change, instead of *defying* them to help you . . .

LORAINE

I want to do everything in my power to do the right thing this time. Nobody believes me!

MICHAEL

Mama . . .

LORAINE

I'm really gonna be well and my old self again after this trip here. I *want* to be like I used to be—and I intend to be. —I just don't know what happened to me along the way.

[*She looks to each of them for corroboration—both are silent*]

I get so put out with myself for thinkin' I'm not able to do somethin' better with my life. I simply *have* to find a remedy for my situation.

MICHAEL
Mama, don't cry . . . please.

LORAINE
Oh hell, I'm not cryin'. You think I want to be here! You don't know what goes on—it gets pretty rough.

TEDDY
Aw Christ Almighty, woman, if you start now, I'm gonna sing "Jingle Bells."

MICHAEL
Daddy!

TEDDY
I'm sorry.

LORAINE
No, I'm the one who's sorry.

TEDDY
Oh come on, let *me* be sorry.

MICHAEL
Daddy, please . . .

LORAINE
It's just gonna take time—and plenty of it. But that's what I do have plenty of.
    [*Brightly*]
One thing for sure—it can't be for always.
    [*Neither answers for a moment*]

TEDDY
Here comes the nurse.

LORAINE
[*Looks to* MICHAEL]
Already?

MICHAEL
Goodbye, Mama.

LORAINE
Goodbye, my angel. Drive careful and have fun and go back to school and study real hard. Are you learnin' some French?

MICHAEL
I'm in third year.

LORAINE
That's good. Most everything I read has a lot of French words in it which, of course, leaves me blank.

TEDDY
Merry Christmas, Mama.

LORAINE
[*Turns to* TEDDY]
Merry Christmas, Daddy.
[*They kiss each other*]
It's a shame you have to be married to someone like me. I'll try some way to make up for everything I've left out all these years.

MICHAEL
I love you.

LORAINE

I love you too.

TEDDY

I love you three.

> [LORAINE *moves off as the lights dim, to leave only the spot on* MICHAEL, *and the sound of the Gulf surf comes up* . . .]

Scene 4

MICHAEL *joins* TEDDY *on a bar stool. They both have drinks.
In the background a saxophone, wailing some progressive jazz,
replaces the sound of the surf.*

TEDDY

The thing I like about this bar—apart from the view and the
salt-sea air—is that it never changes year after year. Been the
same since the Depression. Makes me feel young.

MICHAEL

Well, they've stopped asking me for my draft card, so *I* feel
older.

TEDDY

If *I* lived up in New York City, my hair'd turn white overnight!

MICHAEL

Heaven may be *your* home, but Manhattan is *mine*.

TEDDY

Well, as long as you're doing what makes you happy. And
even though the magazines haven't yet bought any of your
material, the reports seem to be universally positive.

MICHAEL

It's all Russian roulette, but I love it.

TEDDY
Now tell me the truth, wasn't Father O'Reilly a honey?

MICHAEL
I liked him.

TEDDY
Only one who ever convinced me I could learn to serve Mass at my age.

MICHAEL
I liked him—for a priest.

TEDDY
Oh, I know what must have been going through your mind when I up and write you and say I want you to take an Irish missionary out to a Broadway show and buy him a steak in Sardi's.

MICHAEL
As long as you sent the money, I was delighted.

TEDDY
Mama said when I got his thank-you note, I was grinning ear to ear. You played your hand and your heart perfectly.

MICHAEL
I had a wonderful time.

TEDDY
I'm sure you both had a wonderful time—real people! Keep like that and you'll find lots of happy moments regardless of your down-in-the-dumps periods. Don't lose faith in humanity because you run into a few dogs now and then.

MICHAEL
Yes sir.

TEDDY
[*Takes a sip of his drink. Pause*]
You know that time with Uncle Brian . . .

MICHAEL
What about it?

TEDDY
I never have forgiven myself for leaving you alone in the house with him.

MICHAEL
You didn't know he'd do what he did.

TEDDY
I should have. He did the same thing to me. Worse I think, 'cause I was older. He made me bend over. He didn't do that to you, did he?

MICHAEL
No.

[*Pause*]

TEDDY
How's David Zimmerman?

MICHAEL
Boring as hell, probably. He has a sense of humor like a cement matzoh.

TEDDY
You haven't fallen out, have you?

MICHAEL

No, I just smile and mentally do my laundry list while he bores on. I haven't seen him in a while. He's going to graduate school in Washington.

TEDDY

He knows his stuff though. He's strictly on the ball.

MICHAEL

You liked his parents, didn't you?

TEDDY

I thought they were jam-up!

MICHAEL

I thought you'd like them.

TEDDY

Just don't quite understand why they would choose to send their boy to a Catholic university.

MICHAEL

They're very broad-minded.

TEDDY

Well, I have nothing but praise for them.

MICHAEL

In a crazy way, they remind me at times of you and Loraine.

TEDDY

Please don't compare me with them. They are extraordinary people in my book.

MICHAEL
I just meant . . .

TEDDY
First of all, the Zimmerman family is a family of love—mother, father, offspring, and in-laws. Mama makes the home and runs the family—as it should be. Mr. Zimmerman has money and a fine legitimate racket. I don't know how long he has been making the dough, but it don't take long with wholesale maternity dresses.

MICHAEL
And the Connelly family?

TEDDY
Is a family of . . .

MICHAEL
Of?

TEDDY
Of mother, father, son, in-laws, and outlaws.

MICHAEL
And who runs the family?

TEDDY
Daddy grabs the reins and holds on and tries to run the family. But Daddy is a thirty-year-old loser who has spent his life being smart-alek, Casanova, ne'er-do-well black sheep!

MICHAEL
How old are you?

TEDDY

I was thirty when you were born. The previous ten years of manhood practically a parasite. Quit school, ran away, lived in crap games and whorehouses. Finally, *with* one *in* one. Daddy was a dude.

MICHAEL
[*Finally understanding, at last*]
—The satin bedroom slippers.

TEDDY

Got syphilis, got arrested, got wise. Daddy at this turn is not near as smart as Papa Zimmerman. Daddy doesn't make much money—Daddy doesn't *make* any money, and he meets sweet Loraine. And shows her the ropes and falls in love. And marries her. And for a while life is duck soup. Win or lose. Then the little man comes along and Daddy is really determined to grow up, go to work, and be the breadwinner. But things don't happen overnight.
Daddy is weak as hell through this early period, but as usual, he has his bottle to fall back on. Daddy and Mama don't seem to hit it off any more since he isn't successful at this time—he just don't seem to come up with the bright ideas that the Cap'n does who, by now, is everybody's boy!
The little man is fondled and wooed and pampered by Mama and Aunt Hattiebeth and Uncle Bright Boy, the Cap'n—try to buck that combo with nothin' and then check your blood pressure. Daddy is all wrong—no good, nuts, fanatic, religious crank. Makes no difference, Daddy is determined to bring the little man up to amount to something. Daddy didn't do it right, but he didn't have Mama Zimmerman. Result: interference—no harmony. Outcome: I am still the big louse. Reward: THE KID MADE IT!

[*A moment*]

I feel the difference between the Zimmermans and the Connellys is this: Zimmermans—give proper love, you receive
same. Connellys—if you can't figure out your child's resent-
ment, then check up on Daddy and you'll find out that Daddy
caused it somewhere along the line. I don't blame *you*—but I
will blame you if you don't come through now. Not any time
soon—no rush—just try. I'm glad that you are patient and
understanding with your friends. It's a mark of compassion—
how I love that word. A great and happy virtue. One that if
cultivated can be your source of future great joy; to give and
to give in. Just remember, be good, be meek, be humble, but
don't let no son-of-a-bitch walk over you!

[*A moment*]

MICHAEL
Funny how warm the breeze is for this time of year.
   [*Lights dim. Spot remains on* MICHAEL . . .]

Scene 5

A light comes up on LORAINE.

LORAINE
[*Out front*]
My goodness, this is such a grand connection, you sound like
you're across the street!

MICHAEL
[*Out front; puzzled*]
Where are *you?*

LORAINE
I'm home again!
[*Sincerely*]
And for the first time in many, many times, Michael, I feel like
I can make it on my own and never have to take anything
again.

MICHAEL
When were you released?

LORAINE
Last week. Hattiebeth came and picked me up.

MICHAEL
Why didn't Teddy come for you?

[*Pause*]

LORAINE

Well, that's really why I'm callin' you. He's in Good Samaritan Clinic.

MICHAEL

How bad off is he?

[*Pause*]

LORAINE

Could you manage to get away from your work for a day or two?

MICHAEL

I'm not working.

LORAINE

Do you have the money for plane fare, honey?

MICHAEL

I'll use a credit card. Now listen, Loraine, you hang on till I get there, you hear me?

LORAINE

Don't worry about me. I'm the rock of Gibraltar when the chips are down.
[*Pause. He and* LORAINE *join each other in the playing area*]
He's asleep now so let's not disturb him.

MICHAEL

How are you holding up?

LORAINE

You couldn't kill me with a meat cleaver. All I want is for *you* to get quieted down.

MICHAEL

I'm great. You know, just great. Really.

LORAINE

God, you sound like a Yankee! How do you like my hair?

MICHAEL

When can I talk to his doctor?

LORAINE

He's makin' rounds right now, so it won't be too long.

MICHAEL

Well, what's the story?

LORAINE

Well, his heart is enlarged 29 percent and his ankles are swollen up mighty bad—caused from his heart not bein' able to pump all of the water through his kidneys. So it settles in his ankles. It's called . . . edema. That's the way the nuns explain it to me, I think. They are so educated, and they seem to think everyone else is.

MICHAEL

What do *you* think?

LORAINE

I think it's a serious business. He goes off at times and has a wild look, and then again he'll talk perfect sense. But don't get me wrong, with time we'll get everything back in place and try again to make a happier life.

MICHAEL

Are you . . . are you taking anything?—for your nerves, I mean?

LORAINE
[*Looking him squarely in the eye*]
I haven't had as much as an aspirin tablet!

MICHAEL
[*Gently, but wryly*]
You wouldn't tell me a tale, would you?

LORAINE
[*Defensively serious*]
I'd take an oath!
[TEDDY *moans,* MICHAEL *reacts, gets up, moves over to where the sick room would be* . . . LORAINE *gets up; sotto voce*]
Tiptoe! Tiptoe!
[*Light comes up on another area to reveal* TEDDY *lying in a hospital bed*]

TEDDY
[*Weakly*]
. . . Mama . . . Mama?

LORAINE
I'm right here, darlin'. And guess who else is here.

MICHAEL
Daddy?

TEDDY
. . . Who is that? . . . Son? Son? Is that *you?*

MICHAEL
Yes, Daddy, it's me.
[*He goes to* TEDDY, *kisses him*]

TEDDY
Oh Jesus-Mary-and-Joseph, I must really be in bad shape! Now who called you? Who told you about all this mess?

LORAINE
[*Winks at* MICHAEL]
He just decided he wanted to come home.

TEDDY
That'll be the day.

MICHAEL
How do you feel?

TEDDY
Like cutting a rug.

LORAINE
I know it's the truth.

TEDDY
I'm O.K.—if I could just get my damn kidneys to act. I keep telling myself that if I think about having to have the good sisters catheterize me, I'll pee from now till doomsday. But it seems to have a reverse effect.

LORAINE
That's cause you'd like any woman foolin' with your talliwacker, even if she's married to God.
[MICHAEL *laughs*]

TEDDY
Don't make me laugh. Believe me, it's no picnic.
[*To* MICHAEL]
Always remember, don't kid around with your kidneys!

LORAINE
Oh, I think you're gettin' well. You're actin' mighty feisty!

TEDDY
You been getting my letters and clippings?

MICHAEL
Every one of them.

TEDDY
I particularly like that little poem I cut out of the *Clarion-Ledger*. —"Year after year I plainly see my son is growing more like me— And for his sake I'm just a bit regretful I'm like me so much."

LORAINE
Awwwww, Daddy!

MICHAEL
I love the letters the most.

LORAINE
What did he say? Things about me?

MICHAEL
Sometimes. But only good things.

TEDDY
I'm happy that you said you had a good time in Noo Awlens at the Sugar Bowl—even though it did wind up in a free-for-all in Antoine's.

MICHAEL
Give and give in, isn't that it?—even via airmail.

TEDDY
I was a little concerned about how the tone of my last few sermons might affect you.

MICHAEL

I know my spelling is a washout.

LORAINE

You get that from me. You get all the bad things from me. Of course, you get your artistic nature from me—although Daddy does love pretty things.

TEDDY

I'm not beefing about your spelling at the moment; however, there is no excuse for a college graduate to misspell "forty" F-O-U-R-T-Y. And on a bank check too—that's unpardonable! I am referring to the fact I felt you were being complacent and getting in a rut.

MICHAEL

I'm sorry if I sounded down in the mouth. I'm really very optimistic about my career—even though I can soon paper my apartment with editors' rejection slips.

TEDDY

I'm sure everything will work out on schedule. After all, you've only been out of school a little over a year and a half. With your temperament—if you'd gotten anywhere too quickly— your head might have swelled up bigger than my bladder.

[MICHAEL *and* LORAINE *laugh*]

Mama wants to come to New York as soon as the weather is nice.

LORAINE

That can wait till Daddy gets on his feet again and I get a little more time behind *me*. But we do want to see your livin' quarters—we don't understand what a cold-water flat is. What, no hot water—no heat?

MICHAEL

No, no, it has heat.

LORAINE

Can you cook in one?

MICHAEL

The kitchen's the biggest room. It even has a bathtub in it.

LORAINE

It just sounds godawful to me. Do you have a warm bed?

MICHAEL

Of course, I have a warm bed.

LORAINE

Well, I just want to know what you have in the way of comfort.
To think of you in real need would kill *both* of us.

TEDDY

You get your tact from her too.

LORAINE

We'll just never get used to your bein' gone. If you're not
sellin' your stories, are you doin' anything else? I don't seem
to know anything much about you any more.

TEDDY

Leave him alone, Mama. That's his business. He's a young
man out in the world on his own.
   [*To* MICHAEL]
And on that score I have this to say: If you commit a mortal
sin, say an act of contrition immediately and then go to con-
fession as soon as possible. Gamble if you must, but don't

gamble with your soul. I know you already know this—just a reminder. And now, I think I'd like to try to use the toilet.

LORAINE

Oh good! Let me ring for the orderly.

TEDDY

No. I want Michael to help me.
> [*Pause.* MICHAEL *comes to the opposite side of the bed from* LORAINE; TEDDY *weakly extends an arm.* MICHAEL *takes it, begins to gently pull him from the pillow, slipping his other arm behind* TEDDY'S *back. As* TEDDY *is raised and his feet swing out to dangle in space,* LORAINE *hurries closer to be of assistance. During this,* TEDDY *gives out with a faint gasp and all freeze silently once he is in a sitting position. He is pale as a dead man. Pause*]

Oh Lord, I don't want any cheese—I just want to get my head out of the trap!
> [*There is a moment before both* MICHAEL *and* LORAINE *begin to assist him to stand. Then, as they simultaneously start to lift him, he hesitates and gently pushes* LORAINE *away*]

No, Mama. Michael can handle me.
> [LORAINE *helplessly backs away, then looks to* MICHAEL *and gives him a little sign, as if to say he has her permission to continue.* MICHAEL *kneels to put* TEDDY'S *slippers on him*]

Now ain't this some fine come-off! I never thought I'd hear myself say this—but if somebody offered me cold beer right now, I'd have to turn 'em down.

LORAINE

Don't waste your breath, darlin'. Concentrate on what you're doin'.

TEDDY

Since Mama is looking so sharp, if the Yankees win again, I think we'll surely have to bring her to the World Series, but I see no real reason to wait till then. So as soon as you get back, I want you to get tickets to whatever shows you think we should see.

MICHAEL
Yes sir.

TEDDY
There'll be no trouble selling mine in case at the last minute I can't go. But get those tickets *immediately* and I will reimburse you.

MICHAEL
Yes sir.

LORAINE
It's too cold yet!

TEDDY
Well, Easter is next Sunday. Maybe the temperature will rise with the Lord.
> [MICHAEL *helps* TEDDY *to stand and assists him to move slowly toward the area that would be the bathroom*]

LORAINE
I pray we don't have a dark and rainy day on Easter. All the little children will be disappointed they can't show off in their new spring clothes.

TEDDY
Old Bess Donahue is out here too—supposed to have died last Tuesday, but she's rallied some and they say, if she recovers, she'll be mental the rest of her life. Cirrhosis of the liver, etcetera . . .

LORAINE
Alcohol.

TEDDY
[*Barman's yell*]
Last call for alcohol!
[*He pauses*]

MICHAEL
You wanna stop for a minute?

TEDDY
Hell no! I can't wait to get there—when we do, I just want you
to turn on the faucet and step away a bit so I won't feel self-
conscious.

LORAINE
[*Alarmed*]
Who's gonna hold you up, honey?

TEDDY
I'm gonna hold myself up. I'm gonna hold on to the wall!
[*On his way again*]
Joe Ambrosiani has been serving six o'clock Mass with me
every morning till I had to come out here . . .

LORAINE
On the Q.T., the food in that restaurant has gone down,
down, down.

TEDDY
One morning he said to me, "Does Michael still go to church?"
And I said, "Sho', Joe! Did you ever meet a Connelly without
the purpose to become involved. Well, this is involvement in
the world and concern for the individual *is* the church!"

LORAINE

Slow up, Teddy. You're just bound and determined to overdo it.

TEDDY

All I'm worried about is whether I can *do it* or not.

MICHAEL

We'll soon see.

[*They have arrived at the entrance to the bathroom*]

TEDDY

Now stay out of here, Mama.

LORAINE

Hold on to him tight, Michael. He's so weak he couldn't swat a fly.

TEDDY

Now stand back—stand back for your life!

[MICHAEL *has led* TEDDY *to a point where he faces upstage.* MICHAEL *secures him and steps away.* LORAINE *is a distance apart from them as if she is still in the other room. Pause.* TEDDY, *looking down, then with a horrible, frightened moan* . . .]

OHHHHHHHH!!!!

[MICHAEL *dashes to him, looks down* . . .]

MICHAEL

OH MY GOD, THERE'S BLOOD IN HIS URINE! MAMA! GET THE DOCTOR!

TEDDY

OHHHHHH, NO! —OHHHHHHH, *SHIT!*

[LORAINE *gasps but does not scream; lunges out into what would be the corridor, running* . . .]

LORAINE
[*In a desperate, ear-splitting whisper*]
Doctor! Doctor! Nurse!

MICHAEL
GET MY MOTHER OUT OF HERE, DON'T LET HER
SEE!

LORAINE
[*Then, farther away, she increases the volume, exiting
hysterically*]
SOMEBODY! HELP! GET A PRIEST! GET A PRIEST!
[*Simultaneous to this action,* TEDDY *collapses backward into*
MICHAEL'*s arms and* MICHAEL *swiftly drags him back toward
the bed, but* TEDDY *collapses to floor, center*]

TEDDY
[*Wildly in shock*]
Aunt Maureen? Don't leave me! I gotta get out of here! Who
are *you?*

MICHAEL
Daddy, Daddy! This is Michael! I am Michael!

TEDDY
Michael? Son?

MICHAEL
Yes! Yes! Your son! Now, listen! I want you to say the act of
contrition with me. Do you understand?

TEDDY
Michael? Michael?

MICHAEL

Yes, yes, I'm here. Now, help me say the prayer. I need you to help me. Come on, now! . . . "Oh, my God, I am heartily sorry . . ."

[*Mumbling in unison, audibly, inaudibly . . .*]

TEDDY

I . . . I . . .

MICHAEL

. . . for having offended Thee . . .

TEDDY

. . . offended . . .

MICHAEL

. . . and I detest all my sins . . .

TEDDY

. . . all my . . . sins . . .

MICHAEL

. . . because I dread the loss of heaven and the pains of hell.

TEDDY

. . . pains of hell . . .

MICHAEL

. . . but, most of all because they have offended Thee my God, who art all good and deserving of all my love.

TEDDY

. . . love.

MICHAEL

I firmly resolve . . .
> [*He stops. Pause*]

TEDDY

> [*Looking up directly at* MICHAEL]

I don't understand any of it. I never did.
> [*He goes limp, and* MICHAEL *sobs and cradles him in his arms and rocks him back and forth* . . . *Slow dim to black*]

Scene 6

Spots come up simultaneously on MICHAEL *leaning against the proscenium with his back to the audience and* LORAINE *seated center.*

LORAINE

[*Out front*]

Dear Michael: Ohh! It's so good to be home again and out of Whitfield. I am gonna put a curl in my hair and work on my clothes and try to look like somebody again. Please take care of yourself, for you are all I have now and I love you more than anything else left in this world.

[*Light change*]

I am back in the A and N building after ten days in hydro, which I wouldn't describe even if the mail from here wasn't censored. But I am feelin' fine. I am also *cooperatin'*. I am gonna stay here this time until I know I can walk out of here and never come back.

[*Light change*]

As soon as I got back home, I decided to let Willy Mae go. I can do what little there is to do around here. I tried to call you but your answerin' service picked up. I know you don't like me to call if it's just for nothin', but it's been so long since I've seen you, I just wanted to hear your voice. I worry about you up there by yourself. You know that as long as I have a place to sleep, so do you.

[*Light change*]

I had a long talk with the doctor today and told him how I

regret all the years of not lettin' him help me in some way to help myself. I am disgusted with myself for not tryin' to see things as they really are. I would certainly hate to ever let myself believe that your and my dreams were all in vain.

[*Light change*]

It's imperative that I sell the house. The upkeep here is just too much. I remember a little doll house on the coast that I always admired. Who knows, maybe it's just sittin' there waitin' for me. Please let me hear from you and please try not to disagree. This place is just too full of memories.

[*Light fades on* LORAINE *but holds on* MICHAEL]

. . . MICHAEL *reaches for his coat as lights come up. He walks into* LORAINE's *bedroom. She is in a negligee seen earlier, but now it is terribly faded and worn—not soiled or torn; it looks as if it had been washed and ironed too many times.*

MICHAEL

I suppose you're gonna tell me you haven't had anything more than an aspirin tablet.

LORAINE

[*Heavily drugged*]
I suppose you're gonna start in on me again.

MICHAEL

I stopped by the garage where they towed the car to have a look at it. It's a miracle you got out of it alive. It's a total loss—you had let the insurance expire.

LORAINE

It's probably for the best.

MICHAEL

Oh sure. Now we can't collect a cent, and we can't even sell it—except for scrap.

LORAINE

I mean, it's best I don't have a car. Good riddance, I say.

MICHAEL

It's a good thing you feel that way—especially since you have been booked and arrested and your driver's license revoked permanently.

LORAINE

And if I *wanted* to drive this minute, I'd damn well do it!

MICHAEL

It's a pity you've never felt that hell-bent about your rehabilitation.

LORAINE

What did you do with the paregoric? It's missin' from the medicine cabinet.

MICHAEL

Never you mind what I did with it.

LORAINE

All right then, don't tell me. I couldn't care less.

MICHAEL

You look like you need a dose of paregoric!

LORAINE

You didn't pour it out, did you?

MICHAEL

You're so full of goofballs right now, it's all you can do to speak.

LORAINE

And if I wanted a dose of somethin', I'd get it!

MICHAEL

What would you bargain with at the drugstore? Warmth and charmth?

LORAINE

I don't need any of your cocky college-degree remarks.

MICHAEL

When you are down to taking paregoric, it means one thing—you're broke. And you can't afford anything better. And times have changed. The days of bribing a black doctor are over.

LORAINE

Black, white, or polka-dotted, the day that money ceases to talk will be the day Atlas drops the ball!

MICHAEL

I also found out a few other details which you forgot to fill me in on.

LORAINE

Go on, chew my head off.

MICHAEL

The lawyers informed me that you told the judge in court that you *deliberately* ran into those people in that pickup truck.

LORAINE

I *did!* They were takin' up all the highway. I kept honkin' the horn for them to move over and let me pass—but they were deliberately drivin' slow and right down the middle of the road just so I couldn't get by. So I fixed them—I stepped on the gas and tore off the back end of that rattletrap!

MICHAEL
You could have killed them!

LORAINE
I was so mad I didn't care! Still don't.

MICHAEL
It's beyond me why those farmers haven't sued.

LORAINE
What the hell do those red-necks know!

MICHAEL
We could have lost this house—which is about all we've got left. And now there's nothing to do but sell it before we lose it, or you let it fall down around you.

LORAINE
And the quicker it's sold, the better.

MICHAEL
Well, it's not going to be grabbed up overnight. I only hope we can get a reasonable price for it.
    [*Directly and cutting*]
One that will allow me to reclaim some of our possessions!

LORAINE
I don't have the slightest idea what you're referrin' to.

MICHAEL
To *this*.
    [*He holds up a yellow receipt*]
It's a pawn ticket, in case your memory needs refreshing.

LORAINE

Where did you get that?

MICHAEL

I found it in your *empty* change purse. I went by the pawnshop
to find out what you've hocked—and the only thing that surprised me is how little was there.

LORAINE

    [*Pathetically concerned*]
Did that old man sell my silver? Time hasn't run out! He didn't
go against his word, did he?

MICHAEL

No. All the flatware is still there and your tea set—and the
candelabra . . .

LORAINE

    [*Greatly relieved*]
Oh thank the Lord!

MICHAEL

What I want to know is, *where is your jewelry!* Your solitaire
and your sapphire bracelet and the diamond wristwatch!

LORAINE

You know I never wear any of those unless I'm puttin' on
the dog.

MICHAEL

And what is all this about a gun, and where the hell have you
hidden it?

LORAINE

The only thing that's been hidden is the paregoric.

MICHAEL
The man said that along with the other stuff you also pawned a gun, but a week or so later you came back and claimed it. *What* gun? And for *what?*

LORAINE
It's just that little pearl-handled pistol Daddy used to keep downtown in the safe. I need it now—for protection!

MICHAEL
Protection from what?

LORAINE
Anybody and everybody—thieves—riffraff! I am a woman alone in a large house!

MICHAEL
I'm asking you again, where is your jewelry? It's not at the pawnshop, it's not on your hands, and it's not on a safety pin in your brassière! I looked! All that's between your tits is a St. Christopher medal.

LORAINE
All of it's in my jewelry box.

MICHAEL
Show it to me.

LORAINE
And that's in the safety-deposit vault at the bank.

MICHAEL
There's nothing in that tin can at the bank!
[*She is trapped and knows it*]

LORAINE

[*Defiant admission*]

They were stolen, goddamnit! And that's all there is to it! I was brutally taken advantage of by someone I trusted. And I don't mean what you think! He and I were friends and that's all. He was a very nice man. Cultivated. Only he was a dope fiend from way back. And he told me he could get me anything I wanted and that I wouldn't have to pay black-market prices. He said he had some connections in Shreveport. And like a fool I believed him. —Don't look at me that way. I can't be to blame every time the wind changes!

MICHAEL

[*Quietly disgusted*]

Ohhhh shit. I feel like beating your brains out just to see if they are really there.

LORAINE

Don't say that, honey. It's already beat me so. But I am not gonna let this throw me. For some reason, I can't help but think it's for the best.

MICHAEL

Is there anything to drink in the house?

LORAINE

I'm sorry, honey, you know I don't drink.

[MICHAEL *starts to laugh—a little hysterically—not much, just a little, and a little sadly, and trails off, shaking his head, as* LORAINE *asks* . . .]

. . . What did you do with the paregoric?

MICHAEL

[*Cruelly*]

I poured it out.

LORAINE
Oh no! You didn't!

MICHAEL
Of course, I didn't. But if you think I'm gonna give it to you, you *are* nuts!

LORAINE
You give me that paregoric or else I'm warnin' you!

MICHAEL
I'm not afraid of you any more. The days of your digging your sharp red fingernails into my flesh and twisting my earlobes off are long gone!

LORAINE
I just wanted you to have some manners and trainin' and be a gentleman. You don't know what the meanin' of bein' whipped is! I was beaten all my life. And so I can tell you one thing, mister, I am not gonna take it from you now. I'll kill you first!

MICHAEL
Give me the gun, Loraine!

LORAINE
You give me the paregoric and I'll give you the gun.
    [*He starts toward her; she flinches*]
Don't you hit me!

MICHAEL
You know you need it. Where's that goddamn gun!?
    [*He pushes* LORAINE *aside, goes to the bureau, tears open a drawer, starts flinging the contents into the air—little glass cylinders clink together and fly out along with lingerie and scarves . . .*]

LORAINE

You stay out of there! Those are my personal belongin's!

MICHAEL

Christ! Every goddamn receptacle in this house has got needles and syringes tucked into it! I bet you've got hypos hidden in the inner springs!

LORAINE

NO!

> [*They both instantly look at the bed, then back to each other. Suddenly she makes a dash for the bed and scampers into it, up against the pillows and headboard*]

MICHAEL

> [*Quickly coming toward her*]

Get out of that bed!

LORAINE

You keep away from this bed!

MICHAEL

Get off that bed or I'm gonna pull you off bodily!

LORAINE

You do and you'll regret it!

MICHAEL

> [*Quickly moving closer*]

You heard me.

LORAINE

Don't you come another step!

MICHAEL

You think I'm talking to myself? Get away from those goddamn pillows!

[*He lunges at her*]

LORAINE

DON'T YOU TOUCH ME!

[*He starts to rip the pillows away; she recovers, fighting to
prevent his getting the gun. The gun now flashes into view
and they are both desperately struggling for it*]

MICHAEL

Give me that fucking gun!

LORAINE

Let go of me, YOU PRICK!

MICHAEL

LET GO!

LORAINE

NOOOOOOOO!!!

[*Screams*]

IT'S MINE! GIVE IT TO ME AND LET ME STICK IT
IN MY MOUTH AND PULL THE TRIGGER!!!

MICHAEL

[*Struggling with her*]

If only you had the guts, you cunt! If only you had the nerve
to kill your worthless self on your own time! But you won't!
AND I'M NOT GOING TO LET YOU DO IT ON MINE!

[*The gun goes off! She screams again and he finally manages
to wrench it from her hands. She collapses back onto the
remaining pillows, sobbing hysterically*]

LORAINE

I wish I was in hell with my back broke!

MICHAEL

[*Removing the bullets*]
You *are* in hell! And I am now going to escort you to Whitfield.

LORAINE

[*Springing upright*]
NO!! You wouldn't do that to me!

MICHAEL

[*Puts the bullets in his pocket, tosses the gun into the open bureau drawer*]
Oh yes I would and *am*—just as soon as I pack a few of your precious garments, of which you take such remarkable care.

LORAINE

[*Forcefully; getting off the bed*]
Oh no! Oh no, Mister Big Shot! You're not gonna put me behind bars and walk off to New York City on *my* allowance.

MICHAEL

[*Gathering articles of clothing*]
You have no allowance! You have run through everything he left you and you're in debt over your head. And so am I. I haven't got a nickel to my name. I'm going back to New York the way I came—on my credit card—my *bad* credit card!

LORAINE

Your daddy would die.

MICHAEL

My daddy *is* dead.

LORAINE

Poor Daddy.

[MICHAEL *has now retrieved a small suitcase and is stuffing things into it*]

MICHAEL

Poor Daddy, my ass.

LORAINE

He was good!

MICHAEL

He was a maniac!

LORAINE

Don't you say a word against him!!!

MICHAEL

Don't you defend him to *me!* And damnit, put your clothes on!

LORAINE

You can't take me anywhere! You've gotta have the papers!

MICHAEL

I've *got* the papers! And I've got the fifty dollars—I borrowed it from Willy Mae. And I've got a tankful of gasoline. And when I see those big green trees on either side of the road, I'm gonna let out a yell that'll shake the ghost of Teddy Connelly!

[LORAINE *is wide-eyed with fright. She runs in panic.* MICHAEL *races after her, clutches her*]

You come back here! I'm through having you run out in the street half naked. So help me God, if there is one—this is the last time I'm dragging you to the goddamn loony bin!

LORAINE
[Breaks]
Please, Michael! For God's sake, show a little mercy.

MICHAEL
[Releasing his grip hostilely]
My mercy has run out. We are fresh out of mercy, and understanding and patience, and forgiveness forever!

LORAINE
[Terrified]
They'll put me in hydro! You don't know what that means!

MICHAEL
I did not put you in this position.

LORAINE
[Lashing out savagely]
Well, your life is far from perfection!

MICHAEL
GET DRESSED! OR I AM GOING TO DRESS YOU!

LORAINE
[Instantaneous switch to a soft, pleading tone]
Please, Michael! I beg you.

MICHAEL
There's no use begging me!
    [LORAINE finally realizes that he is serious . . .]

LORAINE
Then please . . . please have the charity to give me the paregoric. If you don't, I'll go into convulsions before we get there.

MICHAEL
No! You're not getting it!

LORAINE
[*Desperately sincere*]
Believe me, baby. I'll be in acute withdrawal before we're even halfway there. And God knows what I'll put you through. And . . . and . . . Michael . . . I'm scared. This time . . . If I go into a coma—I'm scared I'll die.
[*Quiet. Pause. He goes, picks up* LORAINE'S *Kodak, opens the back, and lets five small bottles of paregoric fall out onto the mattress*]

MICHAEL
That's all there was left.
[*Before the words are out, she has pounced upon the bottles, tearing one after another open, drinking them dry, and letting them fall to the floor until all five empties lie scattered at her feet. Pause*]

LORAINE
I thank you.
[*She slowly gets up from the bed*]
What shall I wear?

MICHAEL
Whatever you'll be comfortable in.

LORAINE
I wanna *look* decent.
[*She starts to wander off to her clothes closet*]

MICHAEL
Mama . . .
[*She stops*]
. . . I apologize.

LORAINE
[She retrieves a dress from the debris on the bed]
I know you don't mean it, darlin'. I know you're sorry. And if you can believe it, I am too. Here. Help me get this off.
[He helps her out of her nightgown and into her dress]
. . . Please believe me when I say I never meant to hurt you —of all people. Or anyone, for that matter. And I *want* you to get as far away from all this as you can. There's no need of you grievin' your life away over my shortcomings.
[He turns away. She goes to the living-room area]
You didn't mean what you said about Daddy, did you?

MICHAEL
Of course not.

LORAINE
I didn't think so. We all say things when we're aggravated we don't really mean at all.
[MICHAEL returns to stand before her with a pair of her shoes]

MICHAEL
[Extending them]
Put on your traveling shoes, sweet Loraine.
[She hesitates. He kneels and slips them on her feet]

LORAINE
[Looking around]
Well. That's the second bullet in that wall. Whoever buys this place is gonna think there was a firin' squad in that room.

MICHAEL
They'll just know *we* lived here.

LORAINE
I guess you're right. If I only had the ability to put into words

what I would really love to say to you. It's times like this I realize how insecure and no good for nothin' I really am.

MICHAEL

Hush, Mama. I won't hear a word of that.

LORAINE

I know it may sound peculiar, but this living room has always been more like a ballroom, and if you squint your eyes, you would think it's the beach. Let's just sit here a moment with our eyes shut and pretend that a lovely breeze is blowin' in off the Gulf. If we think about it, that's where we spent our happiest moments. We had only moments of happiness—and they were always on the Gulf Coast—but they were enough to make up for a lifetime.

[*Pause*]

Do you mind if I sing? It might lighten things.

MICHAEL

Be my guest. Sing to your heart's content.

[LORAINE *starts to sing gently* "Red River Valley" *as the lights dim, till only a spot remains on* MICHAEL . . .]

LORAINE

Michael?—Michael?

MICHAEL

Yessum.

[*Spot fades to black*]